Praise for Pieces of Someday

"Great memoirs are characterized by the quality of their attention to the universal, quotidian experiences of human life—and the honest, courageous exploration of the self, proverbial warts and all. By this measure, Jan Vallone's memoir, *Pieces of Someday*, is a wonderful addition to the literature. Vallone's narrative gift—by turns lyrical, funny, and raw—combined with her awareness of grace, provides the "fusion and repair" that render a life whole and meaningful. Read about her life and gain new insight into yours."

—Gregory Wolfe, editor of *Image* and author of *Intruding upon the Timeless: Meditations on Art, Faith, and Mystery*

"I enjoyed *Pieces of Someday* so much, I read it twice. The first time I inhaled it, and the second time I went back to admire the artistry and savor each scene. Jan Vallone is truly a gifted writer, and I fully enjoyed the immersion in her colorful, aromatic and poignant reflections. Her feisty spirit, probing mind, and buck-naked honesty are arresting. And her way of telling the story, folding back layers of time and perception, is captivating."

—Barbara J. Elliott, author of *Street Saints: Renewing America's Cities*

"Jan Vallone's memoir is something rare: a story that is deeply personal, and yet one that will resonate with countless contemporary women seeking some deeper gratification beneath the surface of success. Her candor and her pointillist's eye for detail emerge in writing crafted with power and precision."

—David Sobel, editor and writer, instructor at Eugene Lang College, The New School

"I laughed, I cried—mostly I related. *Pieces of Someday* is unflinching—a heart-wrenching memoir about one woman's battle against expectations. With this book, Jan Vallone brings light into the world and shows you've got to believe in people."

—Isla McKetta, editor of *Forum Magazine*

"*Pieces of Someday* is a beautifully-written account of fathers and daughters, teachers and students, successes and failures—the wonderful offspring of what Vallone calls her 'dominant ponder gene.' Holding up a defiant hand against the cynicism that has come to mark so much of America's story, she insists that the greatest success may be measured, not in the things we accumulate, but in the lives we touch."

—Les Lamkin, teacher, author of the fiction collection *Happiness is a Dead Wife*

"A gripping and earnest account of one woman's search for what truly matters in life."

—Roxana Arama

"*Pieces of Someday* invites us to savor the intimate beauty of seemingly ordinary moments and trust that all the disparate pieces of our lives and all our various wanderings can bring us personal fulfillment and also serve the world. Through her poignantly told story, Ms. Vallone demonstrates that one's unique personal call from God is not reserved for someday, but is revealed in the everyday."

—Fr. Mike Fones, O.P., co-director of The Catherine of Siena Institute

"I was at once seized by this book. The story of Vallone's life in New York, Seattle and Italy is one to which every hungry reader can relate. Vallone's work is joyful, impassioned, and endearing; her book is truly a celebration of her life as a teacher, her reverence for tradition, and the embracing of multicultural paths."

—Julie Greene, author of the memoir *This Hunger Is Secret: My Journeys through Mental Illness and Wellness*

"Vallone's life blooms on these pages like the flowers in her garden—fragrant, colorful, real."

—David Berg, computer technician and musician

"*Pieces of Someday* is an irresistible and important look at one woman's choices. From the dutiful path of Catholicism and law to the passion and emotional risk of teaching English in a yeshiva, Vallone captures the poignancy of her life with fine prose that takes the reader to the heart of each event. She is a born teacher and her writing conveys this dedication with a fluid and captivating style."

—Ann Keeling, writer and teacher

"An authentic and inspiring memoir of love, hope and self-discovery."

—Teresa Daggett, lawyer, Quantum Law, PLLC

"With courage and humor, Vallone tells of her struggle with prominent ideas about career, religion, beauty and gender roles. *Pieces of Someday* takes on the myth that life is a vector; to read it is to appreciate the beauty and imperfection of our own stained glass lives."

—Priya Keefe, writer/performer of the CD *From the Lips of Town Criers*

Tossing coins, Trevi Fountain, Rome

Pieces of Someday

A MEMOIR

Jan Vallone

"Joyful, impassioned and
endearing—a memoir celebrating life."
—Julie Greene

GEMELLI PRESS

Published by Gemelli Press LLC

9600 Stone Avenue North

Seattle, Washington 98103

Cover design © Cristina Rinaldi

Typeset design © Enterline Design

ISBN: 978-0-9821023-5-0

Printed in the United States of America.

To order additional copies of this book

or for more information please visit:

www.gemellipress.com

GEMELLI PRESS

On Truth

This book is a memoir, which means it's truth based upon memory—my recollection and interpretation of occurrences and emotions. Now, memory is personal and changeable; unconsciously it modifies the past, which means that my recounting of a moment will be different from anyone else's, even those who were there; each of our truths is unique. And since memory by its nature lapses, sometimes in writing this story, I have found it necessary to fill in minor details or to approximate dialogue.

Then there's the matter of privacy: some people cherish it greatly. Recognizing that, I have altered the names of some individuals, institutions and places mentioned in these pages. But I have not altered names of immediate family members, misrepresented salient venues, misquoted any person's writing or fabricated people or events.

In short, I believe this book is as truthful as a conscientious memoir can be.

Jan Vallone
January 4, 2010

This Book is Dedicated to

Josephine and Peter J. Vallone
and Mark, Cristin and Sean.
I love you all.

Thank You

Roxana Arama, Teresa Daggett, Bea Gates, Elena Georgiou, Les Lamkin,
Jocelyn Lieu, Gwen Mansfield, Sean Roberts and David Sobel—
for your encouragement and invaluable comments;

Cristina Rinaldi—
per la tua amicizia e la piu` bella copertina che io abbia mai visto;

Jason Enterline—
for your beautiful print design and limitless patience;

Barbara J. Elliott and Fr. Michael Fones, O.P.—
for assuring me that even I have gifts;

Rick Hamlin, Bill Hesse, Kari Hock, Nan Holmes
and Steve Kaufman—
for opening doors;

Fr. Tom Kraft, O.P., Jesson Mata and Fr. Daniel Syverstad, O.P.—
for personifying love, hope and perseverance;

Akiva, Chelsea, Jack, Mira, Shoshana G., Shoshana R., Zach
and the writers of Goddard Port Townsend—
for sharing your words and light.

Pieces of Someday

Prologue

*There are different kinds of spiritual gifts but the same
  Spirit;*
There are different forms of service but the same Lord;
*There are different workings but the same God who
  produces all of them in everyone.*
*To each individual the manifestation of the Spirit is given
  for some benefit.*
*To one is given through the Spirit the expression of wisdom;
  to another the expression of knowledge according to
  the same Spirit;*
*to another faith by the same Spirit; to another gifts of
  healing by the one Spirit;*
*to another mighty deeds; to another varieties of tongues; to
  another interpretation of tongues.*
But one and the same Spirit produces all of these. . .
*For in one Spirit we were all baptized into one body,
  whether Jews or Greeks, slaves or free persons, and we
  were all given to drink of one Spirit.*
                              —*1 Corinthians 12: 4-11, 13*

· · · · ·

*Rabbi Judah the Prince would say: Which is the right path
  for man to choose for himself?*
*Whatever is harmonious for the one who does it, and
  harmonious for mankind.*
                              —*Pirkei Avot: 2.1*

Calling

May 2008

W hat am I doing here this morning, sitting in a church when it's not Christmas? Sunlit clouds, breeze tinged warm, pink clematis scent—I should be out in my garden. For twenty years I've driven by this place, felt the pull of its wine brick walls and copper steeple. Cornerstoned when my grandparents boarded steamships from Palermo, until now this Seattle landmark never called me in. Possibly its name has been the dissuasion—Blessed Sacrament—saccharine as *raindrops on roses*. Or maybe I still don't understand what a blessed sacrament is.

I survey the strangers gathered in the pews—the quartet of moonfaced girls sitting to my right, their U.W. sweatshirts nubby, needing bleach. They whisper, nod and smile—smooth skin, glossy hair, teeth straight and white. To my left is a gray-haired woman in a hand-me-down cap. It's crocheted, studded with buttons—S' mores Not Wars, Hope Obama 08. Crinkly eyes, liver-spotted cheeks, whisker-stubbled chin, she's transfixed by something on the altar. Jesus crucified? Must be. For here, except for the icons, there's a howling scarcity of men. Only Saints Dominic, Jude, Thomas, Francis, stand niched and polished around us. They watch in mahogany silence, this nave of waiting women, this raftered ark with its faint incense smell.

The walk from my house to this church took less time than I'd imagined, past Cowan Park, the student rentals reeking weed, Pierced Hearts Tattoo, the Wayward's coffee cloud. Past the bungalow with the big magnolia and the homeless teen crouched in the doorway of the bar who reached his palm out to me, cut my core with steel-gray eyes. If I'd had the courage of a year ago, I would have stopped before him. I would have taken him by the hand. I would have pulled him to his feet and urged him to come along, for it's the church's Called and Gifted Workshop that's drawn me. My kids are grown, away at college, last June I lost my job, and I can't seem to find a new one, three decades of work be damned. Is this what middle age means? Superfluous, obsolete? Which is why I left the boy behind. The blind, leading the blind.

The last time I heard about callings, I was probably twelve years old. Every Wednesday afternoon, Tina Rinaldi and I left public school early to go to Catechism on a church bus. I was embarrassed by the attention this practice garnered at our mostly-Jewish junior high, but also grateful that at least at Saint Christopher's, I was counted among the flock. I remember the day Sister Agnes chalked *vocation* on the blackboard, her sprawling, spidery script, rosary-crucifix-swinging habit hip. She explained that vocation was a calling, the work God created us to do. Each of us would have one, each would be unique, and God would give us the necessary talents—*gifts*—to do it well. We needed to listen for God's voice very carefully, so when he revealed our callings, we would hear.

Through the years I've often thought about those teachings, sometimes with anger, others with longing, always with sadness. I'm old now, Sister Agnes, when will my revelation come? And how will I recognize God's voice? Are my dreams signs of my calling? Or are they just sinister specters rising from the refuse of my childhood? After all, both the Crusaders and Al Qaeda thought they were heeding the call of God.

The light shifts in the church. Rainbowed sunbeams moving through stained glass draw my eyes to the panes above the altar. Jesus in white robes, golden crown upon his head, raises an amber chalice emitting a nimbus of flames. The Virgin Mary prays in turquoise; Saint John clasps a scarlet book. Then a host of swirling symbols— an emerald scale, a stringed harp, a silver sword. A pair of candles, a yellow star, a nodding lily. A russet heart, a rising sun, a purple fish. A pelican pierces her breast, splay-beaked fledglings at her knee.

When I was a little girl, my cousin Angela told me life's a circle, and looking across the generations, I suppose she was right. We are born, have children—at least those who can and want to. Then we die and, theoretically, our children carry on.

But I pictured life as a vector, one leading to a place called There. To arrive, I'd have to work hard—that's what my father said. And I'd also have to be good, which I knew meant do as I was told *thy kingdom come, thy will be done, on Earth as it is in Heaven*. Then one day I'd finally be There, in an Oz of endless sunshine, love and reward where I could remain for all time.

Now life seems neither circle nor vector. Those shapes are too simple, one-directional. So I've tossed away both paradigms, and that's just fine. I did well enough in math, but only through resolve and application. Numbers, graphs and figures don't come naturally to me.

Life, it now seems, is a stained glass window composed of bits of translucence and opacity—fragments of yesterday, chips of today, pieces of someday, soldered with time. Some jewel-like and whole. Some fractured by the weather. Others fallen from their leaden frames. Only fusion and repair complete the image and allow us to make out the picture. Am I a scale, a harp, a star? A candle, anchor or heart?

And what about tomorrow?

Turning Home

July 2000

*M*y husband Mark and I strolled arm-in-arm down a cobbled street in Rome. A late night breeze drifted pleasant and warm—the last breath of a hot summer day—and stars pulsed like fire-flecks in the sky. Stylish cliques and couples clustered over tables of outdoor cafés, faces glowing in lamplight, voices a polyphony of Italian, German, Dutch. They lingered over espresso, swigged crystal shots of *grappa*, shared clouds of *tiramisu* as their bow-tied waiters buzzed. I sighed. "It's been a great vacation."

Mark squeezed my elbow. "I think so too."

We turned down a side street in silence. It *had* been a great vacation. Rolling drives through fields of sunflowers, trellised grapevines, silver olives. Lovely walks through Pienza, Florence, Gubbio. We'd pondered airy basilicas vaulted cobalt, scattered with stars, swum the Tyrrhenian's aqua warmth. We'd binged on *Bolognese*, sipped glasses of *Brunello*, shopped for *maiolica* vases glazed amber, blue and rose.

Why didn't we fight on vacation? Why didn't I brood and grumble? Why didn't I weep and rage, my *modus operandi* at home?

Home—Seattle. The thought of it made me cringe. Born and raised in New York, I'd not adjusted in fifteen years. We'd moved there on a whim, seeking a land of milk and honey, where the weather would be mild, the houses charming and affordable. Where we could start a family and have plenty of time to play. Where I could quit my job as a lawyer—one I never enjoyed—and find things I'd love to do, like gardening, or teaching maybe.

Mark—lucky for him—had blossomed in Seattle. He'd flourished at his law firm, cultivated well-heeled clients who gave him cabernets and praise. Never looking back, he'd traded Yankees for Mariners, Brooks Brothers for fleece, Stairmaster for cycling. He'd lost his New York pallor, become robust.

Meanwhile I'd withered. In Seattle I burrowed through the years like a shrew-mole through the mud. I surfaced only to complain about the weather, our house, my job.

Dr. Llewen called it S.A.D., a depression caused by lack of sunlight resulting in low serotonin. She said victims suffer melancholy, petulance, anxiety, social strain. Since evolution has optimized humans to receive equatorial light, S.A.D. is common in northern latitudes and climates with cloudy skies. Dark-eyed people like me are genetically predisposed, while blue-eyed people aren't; their irises take in more light.

Just my luck. Seattle is rain on cedars, umbrella-broad mushrooms, coats in July. A land of mackerel skies, moss dangling from hemlocks, slugs slinking on slime. No wonder Scandinavian immigrants had chosen to make it their home. They could gaze out their log cabin windows, see the Olympics, misty, cold, rising from fir-clad foothills and dropping into the sea. They could work as fishermen and lumberjacks as they had in the Old World, keep their woodstoves stoked and fired nine months a year.

But while Andersens bumped on covered wagons searching for faux fjords, my grandparents retched in steamship cabins praying for mock sciroccos. They longed to stroll boardwalks on Sundays, see the Atlantic, swelling, gray-green, stretch from sandy coasts like those in Sicily. They aspired to learn city trades they'd never done before, but hoped to grow tomatoes in their gardens all summer long. So my mother's side, the Errantes, opted for Coney Island, and my father's, the Vallones, chose the Lower East Side. And when my parents, like so many others of their generation, decided to leave the city, they chose the shore of Long Island. I grew up in Baldwin Harbor on the beach.

Dr. Llewen recommended a light box with fluorescent full-spectrum tubes. I should plan to sit before it mornings for an hour, about a yard away. I should keep my eyes open for the session, never look straight at the bulbs. For as long as I lived in Seattle, I should lap artificial light, Tang instead of fresh-squeezed.

I told Mark about S.A.D. that night at dinner, poking *penne* round my plate. I explained the symptoms and the science—lawyer talk requires evidence. As I spoke, Mark rolled one hand in the air before his chest, meaning *Please expedite.* So I said, "I need a special light box."

His blue-eyed verdict: "Seems to me you need a shrink."

Shrink, a cringe-worthy word I'd once read was short for *headshrinker,* a primitive tribal healer who sundried the heads of slain foes. As soon as Mark uttered the word, it achieved its ancient effect. I shriveled like a raisin, renounced my faith in the box, resolved to raise my serotonin through the sheer force of my will.

When I was a little girl, my favorite movie was *Miracle on Thirty-Fourth Street.* Maybe that's why the house we'd purchased only worsened my stormy moods. In the film, six-year-old Suzie hopes her mother Doris will marry Mr. Gailey. She wants to have a real family, one including a father, and move away from Manhattan out to Long Island. She yearns to live in a house, have her own room, a backyard with a tree swing. Still, she never tells her mother. Instead, she asks Kris Kringle, her mother's friend and Macy's Santa, to grant the wish for Christmas. But beneath the tree Christmas morning, Suzie finds only toys, and Kris, who's there for the holiday, sees she's sad. "I'm sorry, Suzie. I tried my best, but. . ."

Suzie shakes her head. "You couldn't get it because you're not Santa. You're just a nice old man with whiskers, like my mother said, and I shouldn't have believed you."

Doris overhears her daughter, kneels, looks into her eyes. "Suzie, I was wrong when I told you that. Just because things don't turn out the way you want them to the first time, you've still got to believe in people."

Later Christmas Day, Gailey's driving home from a party, lost in suburban Long Island, Doris consulting a map. Suzie's gazing out the backseat window. "I believe. I believe. It's silly, but I believe...Stop! Mr. Gailey. Stop!"

Gailey slams the breaks and Suzie leaps from the car. She runs towards a small Tudor house, yanks the door open, races inside. Gailey and Doris follow, and Doris calls, "You shouldn't run around in other people's houses. You know better than that!"

Suzie calls down the stairs: "But this is my house, the one I asked Mr. Kringle for. It is! I know it is! My room upstairs is like I knew it would be! You were right, Mommy. I kept believing. Look, there's even a swing!"

Standing before the fireplace, Gailey smiles, takes Doris in his arms. "The sign outside said it's for sale. We can't let her down."

They kiss to crescendoing "Jingle Bells".

But our house did let me down. One hundred years old, badly remodeled in the seventies, it was far less than a dream house, far more than we could afford, even though we'd lived in a starter house, saved our money for fourteen years. Had she lived to see it, my mother would have called it a dump, which is how I described it myself. Thank God she would never know her savings had footed the bill. Leaky roof, smoking fireplace, sinks backed up with raw sewage. Cracked plaster, battered floorboards, creaky stairs without a balustrade. Although some of the windows were lovely—original fir-framed diamond lights—many were metal replacements, and almost all of them sagged. One night our neighbor Steve cocked his head while drinking a glass of wine, "Hey, is that window crooked, or is it the *Sangiovese?*"

Worse, the place seemed unsafe. Whenever I blew dry my hair, the basement fuses blew out. And our electrician almost blew up while renovating the kitchen. "Christ!" he shouted one morning after taking off an old switch plate. He pulled out yards of wire—braids of yellow, orange, black—their copper ends frayed, sparking, a Flintstones fix-it job:

Wilma, kneading dough on a boulder: "Fred dear, this kitchen needs more light!"

Fred, clubbing a hole through the wall: "There you go, Hon. All done!"

But Mark thought our house a smart move: a rare listing close to Roosevelt, known as one of few decent urban high schools, our kids Sean and Cristin eleven and thirteen.

Still, I bucked from the moment the seller accepted our offer. Every morning before we moved I poured Mark his coffee: "*Please,* cancel our contract." Midday I called him at work: "I just can't live in that dump!" Evenings I hissed over supper: "Fine! Move there with the kids!" At night I sobbed in our bed. But Mark refused to rescind; our agent was his law partner's wife, our deposit nonrefundable, five figures.

The day of our house closing brought no miracle, no kissing, no jingle-bells crescendo. Instead, I sat at a conference table with a view of Elliott Bay, ferries clipping back and forth. I wished I could hop on the *Tillikum* and pilot it to Hawaii or parachute on the *Puyallup* and sail it back to New York.

Meanwhile, Mark was signing papers, stacking a pile as our agent checked a list. She stood up, smiled with lipsticked teeth. "Almost done!

Just need a few quick copies. Jan, you sign next."

Her high-heels clicked up the hall. Mark pushed the papers across the table and held out his pen to me.

I folded my arms over my chest, hands pressed into my armpits. "I'm not signing. I'm not living there."

Mark clenched his jaw, brain likely re-crunching the numbers.

The agent came back to the room, stood beside Mark. I looked from one to the other—the execution squad. Her red stiletto smile. His ballpoint suspended midair. My heart in the crosshairs.

So I slipped the pen from Mark's fingers, Eve shrinking from God, fig leaf covering desire. I signed the bottom line, ousted myself from the garden.

It's not that I spent much time at home, though. At first, I thought I could handle both career and family, be an archetype of my generation like the woman on T.V. who swore by Enjoli. At sunrise, in my pink bathrobe, I'd flourish an omelette pan: Honey, don't you love the garnish? In my gray skirt suit at seven, I'd hop a cab to the Columbia Tower: Hey, guys, let's make a deal! Evenings, in my lilac cocktail dress, I'd gyrate my body and sing: *I can bring home the bacon / Fry it up in a pan / And never ever let you forget you're a man / 'Cause I'm a WOMAN.*

And 'cause I worked for Turnbull Brewster Dickson, which *The American Lawyer* had dubbed Seattle's lifestyle firm. Not only was it A.V. rated, but its family policies were cutting-edge, so much so that when my kids began grade school, they'd offered me a deal: I could work a seventy-percent schedule for a forty-percent cut in pay.

Part-time contract or no, full-time remained the expectation. Jackie Boyd, a junior partner, had set the standard at the firm. During childbirth, she'd taken a client call and closed a merger, baby in canal. So I racked up tenths of an hour, recording each as my law firm required, so many that I came to measure all of life that way:

Get up, take shower, dry hair.	0.7
Fix fuse, wake kids, make Quaker Oats.	0.7
Feed cat, toss litter, clean kitchen.	0.2
Drive kids to school, head to work, park car.	0.7
Revolve through doors, ascend in elevator, toss coat on chair.	0.2
Listen to voicemail, read email, skim mail-mail.	0.9
Call client, call broker, draft lease.	3.7
Call client, draft non-disturbance agreement.	2.1
Grab coat, descend in elevator, revolve through doors.	0.2
Find car, drive to school, pick up kids.	0.4
Drop Cristin at dance, Sean at soccer, buy groceries.	1.5
Revise promissory note (in car).	1.7
Collect Cristin and Sean, drive home.	0.7
Set table, make spaghetti, sauce, salad; pour milk (with coat still on).	0.8
Greet Mark, toss coat in corner, serve dinner.	0.5
Nudge kids through homework, tuck kids in bed.	1.9
Review file, begin drafting deed of trust.	1.2
Flop into chair, open *Time*, doze on armrest.	0.8
Get ready for bed, slip beneath sheets, sleep.	5.1

In reality, I wound up working full time for sixty-percent pay. Still, Turnbull's managing partner asked me to keep my part-time status hushed; our clients paid hundreds per hour, and if they thought I wasn't wholly theirs, they might defect to Solly Hickley Downs.

Once, I was working on a multimillion-dollar sale of land in Washington, Oregon and Utah when both my children spiked fevers. Cristin, age six, needed her tonsils out, and Sean, age four, a larynx cyst removed. Jackie Boyd dancing in my head, I scheduled concurrent operations, brought my file to the O.R. waiting room. But despite my Enjoli intentions, I stared at the fish tank in the corner. Yellow tangs, purple blennies and orange clownfish darted around a reef. Starfish, snails and hermit crabs burrowed in the sand. And the water bubbled.

Suddenly, the O.R. doors swished open, mint-clad nurses thrusting gurneys through. There went Cristin, tiny and unmoving, wee nose pointing heavenward. There went Sean, inert.

What kind of mother was I?

I opened up my file.

Next day, I stayed at home with my children, a conference call scheduled for ten. Eight lawyers would picture me downtown, working at my office desk. At five to ten, I sat the kids on the couch, popped *Fantasia* in the V.C.R.:

Spotlight 1: The telephone rings. I hand the kids bowls of ice cream, tap *Play*, pick up the receiver.

Spotlight 2: The sorcerer, dressed in blue, orders Mickey to scrub the castle floor. Mickey pouts, the sorcerer leaves, Mickey cops his boss's magic book and hat.

Spotlight 1: I cradle the receiver on my shoulder, pick up a list of lawyer names. "Good morning. Thanks for joining us. First, let's make sure we're all here. Daniel Sheffield? Ben Eisenberg?"

Spotlight 2: Mickey smiles, casts a spell on a broom. It moves, sprouts arms and legs, grabs a bucket, strides to a well.

Spotlight 1: "Dean Wilcox? Jim Strong?"

Spotlight 2: The broom fills the bucket with water, pours it into a cistern. Repeats. Again, again.

Spotlight 1: "George Marvin? Good, all here."

Spotlight 2: The cistern overflows. Mickey bids the broom to stop, but it fills another pail.

Spotlight 1: The kids giggle; I pick up my file. "Ben, let's start with your comments on the mortgage."

Spotlight 2: Mickey grabs an ax, desperately chops the broom to pieces. The bits sprout arms and legs, fill buckets, unleash a tsunami.

Spotlight 1: Dark-light flashes in the room. The T.V.'s flickering, kids bobbing on the couch. "Mommy, fix it! Fix it!"

I grab the remote—*Pause, Play, Stop, Pause, Play!* The T.V. screen goes blank.

"Thanks, Ben."

"Fix it, Mommy, fix it!"

I run to the pantry, lock myself in. "How about your comments, George?"

Kids pounding the door. "Fix it, Mommy, fix it!"

I jab the telephone's mute button, undo it only when I speak, bring the conference to a close, somehow pulling off my ruse.

After, I mended the movie. The sorcerer returns to the castle, raises Jesus arms, breaking Mickey's spell. Mickey kneels and begs forgiveness. The sorcerer points at the gate.

As Mark and I walked, the Roman street narrowed. On either side of the lane rose stucco *palazzi* three stories high, some melon-pink, others lemon, all haloed by lantern light, windows shuttered for the night. I ogled their chiseled stone lintels, their brass lion-head knockers. I breathed in the trellised-jasmine air, wished my children, back in Seattle, were instead asleep in one of them.

A church bell chimed eleven. Mark tugged on my arm. "Our flight leaves early. We'd better head back."

My heart, a moth battering glass. "Oh, just a little more. Let's stop by the Trevi Fountain, throw in some coins."

How I loved the Trevi Fountain, its marble sculptures, waterfall sound. Over its rushing waters, Neptune rides a shell-shaped chariot drawn by a couple of horses, one peacefully trotting, the other rearing wildly. They're the moods of the sea, but they reminded me of my two selves. My tranquil, happy Rome-self. My bitter, miserable home-self. If only I could stay in Rome, I'd always be content. If only I could move from Seattle, I'd never be upset. Ever since my girlhood, I'd been a sap for shamrocks, birthday candles, fortune cookies, found pennies, wishing wells. I needed to visit the fountain, needed to toss in a coin. Legend says anyone who does so soon returns to Rome.

We turned into a *piazza*. In spite of the late hour, it still pulsed with life—lovers holding hands, children eating *gelati*, vendors selling roses, mounted Roman police, all backlit by the Trevi's gods and torrents. As if drawn by a mystical power, we pressed to the oval pool where the hopeful, backs to the water, performed the ancient ritual: clasp a coin in the right hand, make a special wish, toss the coin over the left shoulder, pivot, watch the coin splash.

As soon as spaces opened, Mark fished for coins in his pockets. First, the back pockets of his pants. Next, the side pockets of his jacket. Then, the breast pocket of his shirt.

He shrugged. "Seems I'm out of coins. What about you?"

A fury bolt in my chest, like those that often struck at home. My voice, a thunderclap. "You know I never carry money! Let's just leave— that's what you want! To drag me back to Seattle, knowing I hate it there!"

People turned to stare. I marched out of the square.

Mark trailed me to the hotel. All the way, we said nothing. In our room, I positioned myself. "I'm not going home. I want to stay here— or go back to New York."

He rolled his eyes. "Not this again! My job's in Seattle!"

I pounced. "It's always about you! What about me? You made me move for nothing, nothing at all but rain!"

Mark sat on the bed. He stripped his shoes and socks. "Let's all feel sorry for Jan. You *chose* to move to Seattle. Stop trying to please your father. If you don't like your job, just quit!"

Tears and mucous on my face. "You say it, but you don't mean it!"

How many times had we said this? One hundred, two hundred, three? Usually at my first words, Mark hung his head covering his ears, walked out or opened *VeloNews*. This coiled me even tighter. Our marriage, a cliché. Somewhere I had read that God was invented by humans to satisfy unmet needs—*At dusk, at dawn and noon, I will grieve and He will hear my voice*—and I'd wonder if God was most revered by women whose men preferred sports.

How could Mark be so inhuman? Why couldn't he listen, just once?

I theorized about Mark's behavior, Freuded, Junged, Venused and Marsed. I knew the question was *why*, suspected the reason was "If." A blue-framed copy of Kipling's poem had always hung in Mark's childhood home:

If you can keep your head when all about you

Are losing theirs and blaming it on you. . .

And lose, and start again at your beginnings

And never breathe a word about your loss. . .

If you can fill the unforgiving minute

With sixty seconds' worth of distance run,

Yours is the Earth and everything that's in it,

And—which is more—you'll be a MAN, my son!

One Sunday of our New York years comes to mind. We were

visiting Mark's sister Sue at her Pleasantville center-hall colonial, which the family had nicknamed The Manor. As always, we'd slogged our laundry through Grand Central on the M.T.A., and I'd already stuffed it in the Maytag, helped myself to some Tide. As it churned, we lounged in the den. Sue and Phil—long-married high-school sweethearts, parents of four-year-old Andrew—sat on a floral loveseat, Mark and I on a matching couch, Mark's parents on wing-backed chairs. Pigs-in-blankets exhaled on Lenox, vodka tonics swished all around, and Sue's golden retriever Brooke lay curled within sniffing range. As the conversation segued from Mark's job to Sue's church rummage sale, I studied the print of *Christina's World* that hung over the mantel—a crippled woman sprawled on beach grass dragged her body toward a house, dark hair wisping on a breeze—while Mark's father bounced his towheaded grandson up and down on his knee:

"Little Jack Horner

Sat in a corner,

Eating a mincemeat pie.

He stuck in his thumb

And pulled out a plum,

And said, 'What a GOOD BOY am I!'"

At that, Brooke leapt up barking wildly, Andrew bursting into tears. Mark's father set him on the floor, looked him right in the eye. "Andrew, men don't cry. Now, go to your room till you shape up."

Mark's father, Mark and Andrew. Three generations of MEN. I stood to put the laundry in the dryer. Andrew ran up to his room.

After dinner one night when I was six or seven, my mother tossed me a dish towel: "How about helping me dry the pots and telling me about your day?" This began the ritual that lasted till I left for college and resumed each college break: when my father had fled the supper table toting his *Daily News*, my mother would say, "Talk to me!" and I'd pluck a waffled towel from a hook and join her at the sink. Squirting Joy on a pad, she'd scrub, rinse the suds, pass the pots to me. And I'd buff the copper bottoms in a circular motion—*from grease to shine in half the time*—giggling, gossiping, bawling; whining, probing, guffawing about my teachers, schoolwork, friends.

I suppose, then, it was no wonder: Mark was a moated W.A.S.P. castle; I, an Italian loose cannon, behaviors forged and burnished during childhood we assume are admired by all until we're stirred together in the pot and either combust or melt, unless we seek to bond.

Once though, when Mark and I were fighting, I was the one who walked out. I stood from the dinner table, stormed through the door and climbed into my car. I drove around Seattle for hours, prowling Capitol Hill and Queen Anne. In the semi-dark I parked before a house—brick surrounded by a garden, picket fence dripping honeysuckle, bay window with bits of stained glass.

A woman behind the window was setting a table beneath a chandelier. Blond and slender, she set down a glass, prisming amber light. At one point, she paused beside an archway, and three blond children bounced through, followed by a tall, fit man. She'd probably majored in English, never earned a dollar in her life. She likely ran the grade school P.T.A., received red roses from the principal each June.

The family sat around the table, bowed their heads as if in prayer. Ozzie, Harriet and offspring. Sue, Phil and Andrew.

Was that a retriever bounding in? Why them, not me?

Outside the Roman hotel, a church bell struck midnight. Mark glared at me for a moment, climbed into bed, flicked off the light. Within moments he cooed his pigeon snore. I crawled between the sheets, keeping distance from his fortress back, stared at the shadows on the wall. All night long I seethed: When we get home, I'll divorce him, move back to New York with the kids.

The sun rose early next morning, filling the room with soft light. I glanced at the clock—five o'clock—slid out of bed and dressed. Rummaging through my wallet, I found a quarter, slipped out the room.

Trevi was different that morning. Its cascades weren't flowing, the square was vacant, still, piles of garbage everywhere, no hint of magic at all. I picked my way down a path of trampled ice cream cups, broken beer bottles, crushed roses. I sat on the fountain's edge, my back to the water.

Clanking and screeching round a corner, a bright yellow sanitation truck pulled up and halted. Blue-jumpsuited men leapt from its sides, erupting activity. Some collected garbage, stuffing jumbo plastic bags, hauling them onto the truck. Others unfurled rubber hoses, snaking them over the square, sluicing the stones. Still others thrust brooms and mops. Despite the early hour, the sun was growing hot. Here and there a worker paused, removed his cap, handkerchiefed his neck.

Watching, I shook my head: What a shame these men have to spend their time cleaning up other people's messes.

One man stopped before the fountain. Slumping over his broom, he seemed to strain for breath. Another called out, "*Che c'e`, Claudio?*"

My pulse, beating too fast.

Claudio sat on the ledge, wiped sweat from his temples with his wrist. Several workers rushed to his side. He waved his arm, shooed them away. He hung his head over his knees, propped his forehead with his palms, elbows pressed into thighs. Like Mark, when I yelled.

Disquietude quavered in my chest like leaves gusting in the wind. God, what had I done?

Really, I didn't need Claudio to understand the answer to that question; the ponder gene is dominant in me. What's more, like other

Catholic children, I'd learned the *Confiteor* at seven, first the Latin long version, later the English brief: *I confess to almighty God, and to you, my brothers and sisters, that I have sinned through my own fault, in my thoughts and in my words, in what I have done, and in what I have failed to do.* I routinely brooded my actions, assumed most messes were my fault, imposed sustained, successive rounds of mental self-flagellation. Of course I was aware I'd agreed to move to Seattle. I knew I'd signed our house contract, knew I'd failed to quit my job. I knew this in my quiet moments, knew it while I blamed the status quo on Mark. And I knew I didn't want to live without him at the same time I told myself I did. I hated my enmity and bitterness. I just didn't know how to stop.

After resting for a moment, Claudio stood, resumed his sweeping. The church bell tolled six a.m., so I stood too. I fished the quarter from my pocket, clasped it in my hand, closed my eyes. Okay, Neptune, God, help me clean up the mess I've made.

High over my shoulder I tossed it, turned, watched it descend. Down it came spinning and glinting. It struck the pool's placid surface, ricocheting tiny drops. Then it pendulumed to the bottom, nestling among countless wishes of copper, nickel and bronze.

Part I

And he spoke to them at length in parables, saying: "A
    sower went out to sow.
And as he sowed, some seed fell on the path, and birds
    came and ate it up.
Some fell on rocky ground, where it had little soil.
It sprang up at once because the soil was not deep, and
    when the sun rose it was scorched, and it withered for
    lack of roots.
Some seed fell among thorns, and the thorns grew up and
    choked it.
But some seed fell on rich soil, and produced fruit, a
    hundredfold."

—*Matthew 13: 3-8*

• • • • •

Hillel would say: One who increases flesh, increase worms;
    one who increases possessions, increases worry;
One who increases wives, increases witchcraft; one who
    increases maidservants, increases promiscuity; one
    who increases man-servants, increases thievery;
One who increases Torah, increases life; one who increases
    study, increases wisdom; one who increases counsel,
    increases understanding; one who increases charity,
    increases peace.

—*Pirkei Avot: 2.7*

Flight

I pressed my forehead against the airplane window and stared out into the darkness. Never was a night so black. No stars. No moon. Just the solitary white light at the tip of the airplane's wing pulsing rapidly like my heart.

The cabin was dim and silent. Most of the passengers slept—the mother and child in front of me, the middle-aged priest by my side. Several hours earlier, I too had been sleeping, but in my own Seattle bed, when the telephone cut short my dream. Startled and disoriented, I reached for the receiver and raised it to my ear.

My mother's voice funneled through the phone from Florida. "Honey, your father's in the hospital and might not make it through the night."

I glanced at the photo on the dresser—my father and me at graduation, me in a royal blue gown, black velvet facing, tassled tam. He in a gray hounds-tooth jacket, white turtleneck, bug-eye sunglasses. Both of us are smiling, his hand on my shoulder, Luna moth light.

I sat up in my bed. My mother couldn't be right; I'd talked to my father just the day before. He'd sounded good, strong—excited he could still fly his plane though his cancer had reached one eye. He loved the world from the cockpit—turquoise sea, topaz beaches, emerald fields, like the mosaics we'd seen in Venice churches. "Mom, I don't understand. I thought they had the cancer controlled."

"Honey, his kidneys have failed. Try to book the next flight."

Being his daughter had never been easy, especially during high school. At night, the television babble from my parents' bedroom made it difficult to study, so rather than fight it I let it lull me to sleep.

At four o'clock in the morning, I'd push away my dreams, switch on my nightstand lamp. Air chill on my cheeks, light stinging my eyes, I'd grope for my tortoise shell glasses, seat them snug on my nose. Outside, there would be darkness—a weak streetlamp beam sifting through stirring leaves. Inside, the tick-tock of my pendulum clock was all that I could hear. Mustering self-discipline, I'd reach for the books by my bed— *Pride and Prejudice, Discovering Geometry, Advanced German, Hablamos Español.* I'd spread one open on my blanket, eventually reaching them all, pendulum pounding facts in my brain, impressions from my pen.

My father always told me I had to go to college. While other men may have sung lullabies to their pregnant wives' bulging bellies, my father likely intoned commandments: You must work hard, speak articulately, excel. You must not be like your forebears, unrefined *cafoni.* You must not be a teacher like your mother—no money or prestige. You must be a *professional*—a doctor, or a lawyer like me.

Still, when I was a teenager, doctoring and lawyering never crossed my mind. I loved the Brontës, Dickens, Shakespeare. I loved writing stories, essays, poems. But my father never ceased his incantations. Doctor, lawyer, professional. Doctor, lawyer, professional.

Why do so many parents want to make children in their own image? Why do they give their children breath, set them in life's garden and then deny the fruit? I was my parents' first child, born to be my father, my first sin being female. I'd foiled his plan to name me Perry, the P from *Pietro*—his name, Peter, *Rock*—and after Perry Mason, the lawyer in E. S. Gardner's novels who never lost a case. My father read them all: *The Case of the Substitute Face, The Case of the Reluctant Model, The Case of the Fenced-In Woman, The Case of the Fabulous Fake.*

My father's favorite was *Fabulous Fake.* It begins when a young woman, trembling with excitement, seats herself in Mason's office. She asks him to help her disappear so her parents will never find her. He asks her why she wants to vanish, and she tells him she has reasons she needn't share with him. Mason regards her quizzically. He tells her he won't take her on trust; he has to know who he's dealing with and what, exactly, the score is.

Likewise, my father trusted no one and made sure to know everyone he dealt with. There I am in the family photo album, diapered at age six months, propped on a couch reading *McKinney's Consolidated Laws of New York*. And there I am at nine months, pajamaed with his pipe in my mouth. There I am, in black and white.

Like Mason, my father always knew the score. Every evening after dinner he'd puff his fat cigar, newspaper spread on his lap. "Dad," I'd say softly. "I got my English paper back."

Pulse racing, I'd hand him the paper, a red 98% at the top, and as he flipped through the essay pages obscured by whirls of smoke, I'd shift my weight from foot to foot fantasizing his response: him raptly reading Mr. Kohler's comments, smile exposing his crooked front tooth (which I loved and he hated). Him thwacking my back: "Good job, Kiddo! Chip off the old block!"

But the smoke was never parted by the words I longed to hear. Instead: "A 98? What happened to the other two points?" Chastened, I'd head to my bedroom, and I'd try to find the answer as the sun came up next day.

My father was a perfectionist, and the day I left home for Colgate University was just like all the rest. As my mother, my sister and I waited in my father's Thunderbird, he was still inside our house, jiggling doors and windows, making sure that they were locked. I stared out the backseat window. What was taking so long? We had a day's drive before us, and I was on my future's threshold, poised to stagger the world.

My father came out the front door, locked and jiggled, walked down the path past the red-berried yew I'd hidden under at age five.

"I'm packing away," I'd informed him after he'd forced a spoon of peas into my mouth shouting, "I paid for them! You eat them!" Chatty Cathy rolled in a towel tied Huck Finn-style to a yardstick, I crouched below the boughs for hours (at least it seemed that long to me), hoping parent panic would unfold, that my father would look for me frenzied, maybe even call the police. I wished the sirens would rouse all our neighbors, that my father would realize I was good and be sorry he'd pushed me away. But there was no cop car, no searching, so I sneaked back inside the house when evening grew dark and chill.

Short, built like a tanker, so at odds with his Fred Astaire step, my father scanned the Thunderbird as he reached the end of the path. As he arrived at the driveway, I watched in silence—Come on, Dad, let's go! But instead of opening the car door, he squatted beside it, examining the paint. I could see the shiny scalp beneath his Donald Trump hair nest (emergency hairspray in the glove box), my pulse sprinting as he shook his head: God, no!—he's found a scratch!

Scratches took time. Every time he found one, Earth stopped spinning on its axis. He'd rub his finger up and down the graze to discern the gravity of the injury. He'd retrieve the treatments from the trunk: rubbing compound for serious gashes, polish for minor, and pure cotton cloths. Then he'd:

1. Use one cloth to rub the balm onto the scratch in a circular motion.
2. Let the balm dry into a haze.
3. Use another cloth to buff.
4. Complain.

Why did he care about car dings, but not the dents he made in me? Like Perry Mason's female client, I wanted to disappear.

Instead my father vanished. I was doing well at college, majoring in language and literature ("A waste!" he said), looking forward to the next semester when I'd study German in Vienna with that cutey Vince Kirsch. Only one final remained before late-winter break. Pipes banging in dorm walls, I inserted change into the hall phone, glanced out the window at the night. Ice laced the corners of the panes and snowdrifts glittered in the quad.

My mother's voice: "Helloeeyo."

I smiled, picturing home—my mother with her Jackie O hairdo, receiver clasped in crooked neck, hands rolling meatballs on Formica, Revere Ware on the stove.

"Hi, Mom. I just called Dad about break, but I wanted to say hi to you too."

Utensils clattered in the background. "But he's away on business. You had his number in Florida?"

I pressed my forehead on the window, puffed a frost ring with my breath. "No, he's at the office. Dotty connected me to his speaker."

"But he doesn't fly home until Thursday."

The pane, obscured by condensation. "Mom, Dad told me it's snowing on Long Island, and this morning his car spun out on ice."

In a later phone call he confessed. "I meant to tell your mother sooner."

I paced back and forth in the hall, voice low so my dorm mates couldn't hear me. "You've moved in with somebody else?"

"You'll like her; she reads novels. Her name is Carol Cohen."

I stood stock-still. "You mean she's Jewish?"

In the past, my father had often grumbled, "Christ, Jews are such complainers! As if they own the persecution market! Don't they know for hundreds of years, the Romans fed Christians to the lions?" Now he said, "Yes, she's Jewish. She wants me to convert."

Crumpling in the dorm hallway, I curled round the receiver like a fetus, its coiled cord my last link to childhood. I was aware, yet not aware, of the hum of life outside. I heard but couldn't understand my father's words in the viscous dark. Later, my mother cut the cord when I called her with my father's news, and I emerged to a harsh white light, her shrieks smacking my face.

As I spoke with each of my parents, I pictured them one month earlier, my father's fiftieth birthday. Dressed in a suit and tie, he'd rumbaed my mother round a dance floor, her silky dress swishing about her calves, their smooth, unisoned steps.

How could my father leave my mother? She washed and ironed his shirts so he'd have a crisp one each day. She made his breakfast every morning, always Medalia D'Oro coffee, eggs sunny-side up, toast to lap the yolk. She taught third graders all day to earn the extra income we needed since he practiced law alone, had never clinched a more gainful law firm job. And when he shouted, "Jay, where's my underwear?" as she put on her lipstick for work, she puckered, blotted on a tissue, tossed it in the toilet, kiss-print floating on the water, and rushed to the basement drier to retrieve his boxer shorts.

She screamed throughout winter break at my sister and me, begged us to make him come home, but he wouldn't answer the phone—Peter, the Rock.

Once, when I was reading on my bed, she thrust open my door, silently glared. She grabbed the potted philodendron from my windowsill, hurled it at me. I shrieked, rolled off the bed, ducked-and-covered on the floor. Dirt. Terracotta shards.

"He dumped us when you left for college. You're the only one he loves."

Me, the only one he loves?

I say this with a sigh: I didn't go to Vienna. That was the road not taken, the start of the next thirty years. After break, I returned to campus. Like a caterpillar pupa, I hid myself away, spending most of my time in the library. There, in the shadows, the cells of my unformed wings underwent a rapid mitosis, absorbing all my energy. In the spring, I emerged from my chrysalis. The stimulus? Mating, of course.

I met Dave in a corner of the library. Handsome, charming, funny—who cared if Vince was in Vienna? Zealously pre-med, Dave spent most of his time in science labs. So I threw away my novels and signed up for biology to be with Dave.

Fiji Island Weekend at Dave's fraternity—me in a flowered silk dress that he said made me look like an hourglass. He in a light gray suit, mauve shirt and wide, striped tie. We, necks encircled with leis— yellow, pink, green, white and blue. Dave wrapped his arm around my shoulders, and a brother snapped a photo with a flash.

After supper, we changed into jeans as the tables were cleared from the dining hall. Darkness falling, humidity rising, the smells of sweat and beer. A mirrored ball spun on the ceiling, spiraling slivers of light, the room a rush-hour subway car, a music-throbbing train.

A drunken brother grabbed a microphone: "Time to do the bump!" We dancers raised our arms toward the ceiling, hands catching pulsing light waves, hips thumping hips, singing the Beatles' words: *Baby you can drive my car / Yes, I'm gonna be a star/ Beep beep, beep beep, yeah!*

Yeah, I would—my family's first doctor.

A quick review: language-artsy daughter fails to meet her father's vocational expectations. He leaves home, crushing his wife, who blames their daughter for his affair and begs her to bring him back. Daughter takes up science to snare an aspiring doctor. Says the father of his daughter's transformation: "Kid, *now* you're using your noggin!"

How unwitting we are when young! Had I replaced my wayward father with a boyfriend? Had I conflated the two? Or had I become my boyfriend to be the son my father never had? Or remade myself to lure him back?

Beep beep, beep beep, yeah!

After that, for the very first time, it almost felt like my father loved me. I had no car at Colgate, so he drove me back and forth each term, his rising star too good for the bus. How I loved those road trips! Just the two of us for hours, my father humming to Sinatra's "My Way" on the radio.

During those car rides with my father, I'd stare out the window at the Hudson beyond the Tappan Zee, that Victorian birdcage bridge, Manhattan a black crystal cluster, Catskills on the horizon, and I'd feel a closeness to my father that I'd never felt before. He didn't talk much when he drove, but sometimes he'd pat my hair as we slowed to pass through a toll: "My daughter, the doctor," he'd say, and that meant everything—enough, I thought at the time, to do it his way.

Even so, it was a struggle. I lacked a scientific mind, had taken only geology in high school—no biology, chemistry or physics. But I'd developed self-discipline during those early mornings I'd studied, and by stationing myself in the library, I could do my father's will. I was a fabulous fake; they called me Four-O Vallone (not Three-Eight), inducted me into the National Biology Honor Society.

Still, I had no interest in medicine, no penchant for bodies or blood, and I missed reading novels, writing poems. When Dave, wayward like my father, dropped me for someone else, I transferred to Bucknell University (Pennsylvania—the Independence State) to put distance between the two of us and between me and my parents. But since I was a junior, it was too late to change my major.

I've always been aware of a certain sense of balance everywhere I've lived, as if the building floated on a fulcrum. When I was a little girl, and my parents went out for an evening, I could feel the house corner where their bedroom was tip up while mine sank down, and I couldn't sleep till they returned and our house re-secured to its foundations. Years later I felt this again when my children left for college. And when I myself was at college, my senior year at Bucknell, I experienced a similar sensation when I was in my dorm single room. I felt verve from the room above me, where my friend Dennis delighted in chemistry, keen to become an anesthesiologist. I felt chi from the room beside me, where Sarah reveled in psychology, excited to one day be a therapist. I felt dynamism six doors down, where Valeria chanted in Russian, zealous to become a book translator. I felt electricity from the room below me, where Edward tinkered with circuits, ardent to be an engineer. Meanwhile, I lay lights-off-heavy in my bed, rehearsing confessions in the dark.

"Dad, I know you'll be upset that I wasted tuition and time, but over these last few years, I've discovered I don't like science. I've decided not to take the M.C.A.T. I wouldn't make a good doctor. I'm so sorry."

No, too penitent.

"Dad, I've decided not to take the M.C.A.T. I don't want to be a doctor."

No, too direct.

"Dad, I know you've invested a lot of money in my education, but if it's okay with you, I'd rather not be a doctor. I'm not wild about science."

Damn. I'll take the stupid test.

My father placed a notice in *The Baldwin Citizen* shortly after college graduation:

Janine Esther Vallone, daughter of Mr. and Mrs. Peter Vallone of 3255 Bertha Drive, received the degree of Bachelor of Arts magna cum laude from Bucknell University with a major in biology. Ms. Vallone has been accepted at Georgetown University Medical School.

Those words—a crown of brambles. For, in the end, I decided I couldn't face life as a physician. I enrolled in a med school Ph.D. program, a distinction my father had concealed, and he was no longer humming "My Way".

I remember the bright May day when I found out how my father felt about my career choice—cloudless sky, ivied brick buildings, rhododendrons along the Susquehanna. I was strolling to Bucknell's quad, graduation gown breezing round my ankles, mortarboard in my hand. My parents, who I rarely saw together, walked along beside me, my father in a tweed sports jacket, my mother in her favorite blue dress. They chattered like Ozzie and Harriet, two fabulous fakes. Still, their voices wrapped around me blanket snug.

When we reached the quad's new-mown lawn, professors were lining up for the procession, each with a tasseled tam, the bell sleeves of their robes color-coded with velvet chevrons: royal blue for philosophy, white for arts and letters, golden yellow for science. I gushed at my parents: "Just think, when I get my Ph.D., I'll be wearing a gown like that!"

A flicker in the corner of my eye, an erratic tweed motion—my father pirouetting, chasséing through the milling family corps. I turned to jeté after him, but my mother grabbed my arm. "Let him go!"

I stopped to look at my mother—as if she should give advice! She, who still had him over and cooked him meals for Christmas, his birthday, Easter and Thanksgiving! She, who in his absence called him King Tut.

She tucked a loose strand of my hair behind my ear. "You know how he is. He's angry you gave up medicine. He says the Ph. before the D. means only phony."

With a great deal of shame I confess: I remained in the Ph.D. program just eight weeks. Each day I inched toward the lab bench, bile in throat, and waited for my dissection partner to unzip the plastic bag, unleashing formaldehyde fumes, revealing our cadaver's hair, face, breasts, hips, mons, thighs, feet. With tension-shattering cheek, my partner had named her Bertha after his favorite Baltimore seafood bar ("Eat Bertha's Mussels!" the local bumper stickers read). There she lay, pasty, puckered, turkey-dead, basting in her juices. I imagined she'd once been a mother, sister, wife and friend, imagined she'd had a different name, been beautiful, vibrant, young, imagined her smiling on Thanksgiving as her family gathered round the meal she had cooked for them. I just couldn't manage to carve Bertha's body up.

Dr. Singh, my Ph.D. advisor, asked me in when I knocked at his office. I remember when I first met him at my admissions interview. We smiled our Dale Carnegie smiles, and I told him my passion was embryology, that I believed the human body was Godly art to be revered. I rhapsodized the beauty of the slides I'd seen in college under the microscope—ruby erythrocytes coursing through capillaries, testosterone crystals forming lime kaleidoscopes. Dr. Singh nodded at my words, offered me his hand, tuition and a stipend.

In Monreale, Sicily, there's a cathedral called Santa Maria la Nuova. When I was fourteen, my family took a trip there with my grandfather, who gave us a tour since he knew the church well. The inside walls are covered with mosaics of Old and New Testaments scenes—Eve fleeing from the garden, Moses wandering through the desert, Mary God-bearing in the manger, Jesus crucified. But mostly I recall the central ceiling apse—an enormous Christ Pantocrator, Christ Almighty. Haloed with gilded tesserae, robed in celeste, he blesses with his right hand, holds an open Gospel in his left: *EGO SVM LVX MVNDI: QVI SEQVITVR ME, NON AMBVLAT IN TENEBRIS*—I am the light of the world. Whoever follows me will never walk in darkness. These words seemed curious to me, for my grandfather said if I walked around the church, Pantocrator's eyes would follow wherever I went. I tried it. At the Bishop's Throne, Pantocrator's eyes. By the West Door, Pantocrator's eyes. Throughout the Lay Nave, Pantocrator's eyes.

That wasn't the last time I felt eyes following me. When I told Dr. Singh I'd be leaving Georgetown, he told me he was sad to see me go, that research isn't for everyone and he hoped one day I'd find the right vocation for me. I thanked him, shook his hand and bolted from his office, racing through the hallway, hoping no one would see. But as I ducked down the med school's back stairs, I felt eyes boring through my back. Were they Pantocrator's? Were they Big Brother's? Or were they Big Dad's? For though I claimed my aversion to blood was my reason for quitting Georgetown, I knew I could have stomached anything if my father could love a Ph.D.

I was twenty-two. I wanted to believe that the future still held something for me—career, marriage, children? But I feared it was too late. Each day I prayed for guidance: God, please let me know what to do! And when he failed to answer, I turned to the music of Bruce Springsteen, who never let me down, over and over said: *Someday girl, I don't know when, we're gonna get to that place / where we really want to go, and we'll walk in the sun.*

So what did I do? Déjà vu! I left town to walk in the sun, took off to be with a guy. I moved to North Carolina to be with my Bucknell boyfriend Mark. We'd been dating since mid-senior year; at U.N.C., he was studying law. Yes, Mark would be a professional; maybe he'd marry me. In the meantime, I'd try to find a job.

In Chapel Hill, I combed the classifieds—bank teller at Wachovia, ice cream server at Swensen's, preschool teacher at the Baptist church—but I had no luck. After a month, I managed to line up an interview at Decorating Den. If they hired me, I'd be trained in interior design.

On the day of the interview, I put on a dress and stockings, left an hour for a thirty-minute drive. Following the manager's directions, I merged onto I-40 toward Raleigh, took the NC-751 exit, turned off at Jordan Lake, turned right onto Hope Valley Road. And that's exactly where hope ended. I was shunted onto a detour—red lights flashing, neon men conducting—lost in Oz of winding roads with no wonderful wizard in sight. Long after my appointment time, I was still circling around, until I pulled over and cried.

I took a job in a U.N.C. medical research lab, the only employment I could find. Each day, I made the rounds required of me. I walked to the animal facility, breathed in nostril-twitching air, reached into large steel cages, plucked out six pregnant rats. Prying open my carrier, I dropped my charges inside and hauled them to the lab. There I chose the first one of the day—pink-eyed, squirming, furry, white—pressed her haunches on the counter, felt her heart trilling through her ribs.

"Shhh, so sorry, little one. I'm not going to hurt you."

Of course, I was telling her a lie. I'd syringe anesthetic in her vein, wait till she fell limp, her breath sleeping-infant calm. Then I'd flip her on her back, take a scalpel to her belly, pierce, slit, spread and clamp. I'd extract her babies from her womb. Thumb-sized, velvet soft, pink, they'd yawn and wriggle in my hand. One by one, I'd place them on the platform, stretching each tiny neck, and close my eyes—whack, off with its head. My average: thirty per week.

After, I'd splay the babies' jaws, extract tiny teeth under a microscope, place them in a Petri dish, measure how much fluoride they absorbed. At day's end, I'd return to the still-drowsing mama, inject her with a lethal anesthetic dose. Then I'd toss her body in the trash and wash dishes, test tubes and flasks.

At home at night I cried. How could I murder mothers and unborn babies? My stomach wretched when I saw meat; I could no longer cook or eat it, avoided the butcher at the grocery. And whenever my father called, I avoided mentioning my job. His daughter, the dish-washer. His daughter, the killer, the abortionist.

One night I wandered into to the bedroom where Mark, newly my husband, was propped on the bed studying, law book on his lap. I sat on the corner of the bed. "How's it going?"

"I'm studying."

"What? Let me see."

He turned the book to face me. "Res judicata. You'd find it boring."

I took the book to read:

The federal courts have traditionally adhered to the related doctrines of res judicata and collateral estoppel. Under res judicata, a final judgment on the merits of an action precludes the parties or their privies from relitigating issues that were or could have been raised in that action. Cromwell v. County of Sac, 94 U. S. 351, 352. Under collateral estoppel, once a court has decided an issue of fact or law necessary to its judgment, that decision may preclude relitigation of the issue in a suit on a different cause of action involving a party to the first case. Montana v. United States, 440 U. S. 147, 153. As this Court and other courts have often recognized, res judicata and collateral estoppel relieve parties of the cost and vexation of multiple lawsuits, conserve judicial resources, and, by preventing inconsistent decisions, encourage reliance on adjudication. Id. at 440 U. S. 153-154.

I set the book on the bed. "Jeez, Mark, how can you read that? Seems like Greek to me."

"Told you. Besides, it's Latin."

"Yes, I know."

I've noticed, now that I'm older, that there are certain moments in life that the mind keeps going back to, moments of nonchalant honesty shared with others. Moments instantly forgotten when decisions lie in the balance and a chorus of impostor voices intrudes and overwhelms. Res judicata? Jeez, how can you read that? Seems like Greek to me. Doctor. Lawyer. Professional. Jeez, how can you read that? Seems like... Lawyer. Professional. Moments that, if remembered, could have changed life. But I didn't remember that moment, or if I did, I chose to forget it. All I knew was I'd failed at science, and the doctrine of res judicata barred relitigation of that case. I was ashamed. Ashamed to kill animals and wash dishes for a living, to tell half-truths to my father. Ashamed to have settled for being a wife. So I raised a brand new issue not collaterally estopped. What about law?

One year later—New York University School of Law. There I sat in an amphitheater classroom with ninety-seven other students as Professor Higgins paced at the front, thumbs crossed under his chin, index fingertips pushing into his nostrils. Silent, he pondered something as if channeling the Oracle at Delphi. Suddenly he pivoted, and we students cowered in unison.

I looked down at my book—Please call on Lori Feinstein. She sat at the edge of her seat, hand raised, twitching like a spaniel scenting a hare.

Higgins cleared his throat. "Ms. Vallone, please stand and state the facts of Hadley v. Baxendale."

Thereafter, Higgins was Socrates, and I his Thrasymachus. For the unversed, the Socratic method—at least as practiced in law school—is an academic hide-the-ball in which the professor asks a sequence of questions intended to flummox the student. Each time the student answers, the professor counters, re-questions—query, retort, query—till the student's neurons implode, losing synaptic linkage with her tongue, till her soul begins to recite Saint Thomas' student prayer: *Dear*

God, true source of light and wisdom, give me a keen understanding, a retentive memory, the ability to grasp things correctly and express myself with thoroughness and charm. After which the student stammers, babbles herself into muteness, as Lori Feinstein stretches, reaches, fingertips brushing brass ring. Whereupon Higgins nods at his dupe, utters dryly, "You may sit down," and calls on Lori Feinstein. Whereupon the dupe sits and fantasizes mixing a hemlock shake.

Three years of law school, a whir, grind, threshing machine, where the wheat's prepared for market and sold to the highest bidder, the chaff fed to the cows. Every Monday I wanted to quit, bonfire my books. But my father called me each Sunday, "How's my daughter, the lawyer?"

Oh, that lovely May morning a few weeks before graduation. I lingered in our Murray Hill apartment, light streaming through the windows warming the honey parquet. Across the street, the tiaraed Chrysler Building glinted in a postcard sky. Still in my bathrobe, I settled in a sunbeam on the couch, dialed my father's number, set to make him the proudest dad who'd ever lived.

The receiver clicked on my father's end. "Dad! You won't believe the job I got! Kelley Drye and Warren!"

"Jan? Kelley who?"

This time I articulated, as he still instructed me to do, notwithstanding my imminent J.D. "Kelley Drye and Warren. The firm that's always in the news; they're defending Union Carbide in the Bhopal disaster class action. They're paying me fifty thousand dollars!"

Poh, poh, poh—cigar puffs on the line. "Well, Kid. I guess I should have expected this when you chose that Jewy law school. You're no better than cattle. Real lawyers are beholden to no one—they don't work in big firms. They set up a solo practice."

A solo practice like his.

And that was the first time I felt it: anger towards my father, a throbbing red rage. Through the years, he'd chewed me like cud, gotten what he asked for, spat me out anyway. His daughter, the lawyer, who now realized what she'd done—bound herself to represent a client whose poisons had seeped into the air, killing babies in their sleep. What was I to do? Quit again before I got started? Why did I persist in doing my father's will? Why did I defy my yearnings, flout the scruples in my heart, only to discover I'd misheard my father's voice? All pointless questions. I had tuition loans to pay.

When I'd been a lawyer eight years, my father retired from his practice. Several months earlier, my mother had sold our New York home and moved to Florida. There, she'd purchased her dream house—a tropically-landscaped rambler with a screened pool in Port Saint Lucie, a development sprung from an orange grove overnight. Although they'd been separated seventeen years (as Catholics, they'd never divorced), my mother let my father move in. She assigned him a bedroom and bath at the far side of the house, told him he'd clean them himself, warned him she'd monitor the phone bills and if he called Carol, she'd kick him out.

My parents congregated in the great room, a vaulted kitchen cum family room with picture windows to a golf course, skylights to the sun and moon. It was there that my mother sat, pumping her Singer pedal, making costumes for my children one Halloween the three of us visited. Both Cristin and Sean were preschoolers, and my father had promised to take them trick or treating.

When he entered the room, Cristin was leaning on my mother's knee, wriggling into a jack-o-lantern outfit. Sean was racing round the couch, arms spread wide, buzzing in a bee suit, bobbing pipe-cleaner antennae with glitter-ball tips. "Hey, Papa Pete, look!"

But my father looked at my mother, fingering his neck below one ear. "Feels like I have a swollen gland."

My mother plucked a straight pin from a cluster clasped between her teeth and pierced Cristin's pumpkin-leaf collar. "Maybe you're getting a cold."

"Maybe, but what if it's cancer?"

I prickled like a cactus in the yard. My father was as fussy about his body as he was about his car. Every day he recorded his weight on a yellow legal pad—heart rate, blood pressure, calories from proteins, starches and fat—and announced his scores at breakfast as if expecting applause. I rolled my eyes. "Dad, you're such a hypochondriac!"

Thus, I spurned my father.

"Spurn?" some people might ask, "You call *that* a spurn?" And I'd have to say, "Yes." For although I know that through the generations, children have rebelled against their parents much more dramatically, I had never treated my parents with the slightest condescension or disrespect. The first time I'd chastised my father, several years before, I was quick to chastise myself, but the older I became—maybe the longer I practiced law—the more abruptly I erupted at him.

Once, when my parents visited Seattle, I was stirring a pan of marinara while a pot of rigatoni bubbled, steam wafting to my face. My father watched, leaning on the counter. "You know the secret to good sauce?"

At once I boiled hotter than the pasta. "Dad, I've been cooking for twenty years!"

"Right before you serve it, toss in a cup of *parmigiana*. Delicious! Try it! You'll like it!"

Jaw clenched, I plucked the spoon from the pot, rapped it on the rim, turned off the gas, set the spoon down. "I don't need fat in my food!" And I knew, even as I said it, if he had been anyone else, I'd have scooped cheese in the sauce. Instead, I walked out of the room.

It gets worse. One Sunday morning we were all eating waffles in our kitchen, sun filtering through the windows, daffodils blooming in the yard, our parakeet Kiwi in her cage, twittering in the light. Mark stood up from the table. "Anyone want some more coffee?"

My father extended his cup. "Thanks, I'll take some, Mark."

Sean, belted on his booster seat, maple syrup dripping from his chin, looked at my father. "Papa Pete, why you say Mawk?"

My father turned to Sean. "Excuse me, Kid?"

"Why you say Mawk? Daddy's name is Mark."

"Mawk. That's what I said."

"Mark!"

"Mawk!"

"Mark!"

"Mawk!"

"Mark!"

By then, all of us were laughing, my father searching our faces.

I smothered my grin. "Sean, Grampa grew up in New York, so he speaks differently."

Chair legs rasped against floorboards. My father stormed from the room, a motion so sudden Kiwi wheeled from her perch. She screeched, thrashing her wings, feathers snowing from the cage. But I didn't follow my father to set the episode right as I would have with any other person. Rather, I gathered the plates, shook my head. "Why's he so sensitive?"

I have so many movies in my head, scenes endlessly looping, stirring shame, sadness, remorse. I wish I could cut and splice them to make the endings sweet. I'd edit the New York accent scene, revise the marinara sequence, scrap the Halloween I called my father a hypochondriac. For the lump my father fingered then was cancer.

Non-Hodgkin's lymphoma. Most commonly first symptomized by enlarged, rubbery lymph nodes, then by fever, weight loss, fatigue, night sweats, itchiness, rashes, abdominal pain and swelling. Most typically treated with surgery, chemotherapy, radiation. My father endured it all with equanimity: big shrug, "One of these days, *some little bug is gonna get you*." Colostomy bag and Popeye patch, barrel body shrunken to bones, he drafted a health care directive requiring heroic measures, shellacked his last twelve hairs across his shiny scalp. He played tennis, flew his airplane, enrolled in a memoir-writing class. He also chain-read books: *The Valachi Papers, Bonfire of the Vanities, The Pelican Brief, The Hunt for Red October.* What had happened to the man who'd been vexed by scratches on his car?

One winter afternoon, I found a book on my Seattle doorstep. It arrived in a padded mustard envelope with my father's return address. I tore it open, bemused. In all the years he'd stressed reading, my father had never given me a book except *The Classic Cuisine of the Italian Jews; Memoir of a Vanished Way of Life.* And that was many years before, when I was still in law school. He'd come into Manhattan to take Mark and me out to Lattanzi, an Italian-Jewish restaurant in the Theater District. I ordered *Carciofi alla Giudia*, told the maître d' it was delicious. He said the recipe appeared in a cookbook the restaurant carried, so my father asked for a copy and bought it for me on the spot.

Back inside my house, I slipped my hand into the envelope, but before pulling out the volume, I discovered some folded legal sheets—a penciled two-page letter in my father's dragonfly script:

Dear Jan,

The book is for your reading pleasure and edification. It will give you some insight as to the forces that played upon the southern Italians who immigrated into the United States between 1900 and about 1930. Your grandparents on both sides faced the difficulties of heritage, customs and prejudices placed before them as hurdles to acceptance and assimilation. You will get some ideas as to why the Vallones looked upon me as a maverick with my head placed slightly askew upon my shoulders, especially Grandma, who apparently felt I was ungrateful and a snob because I did not pursue tailoring. They started grooming me when I was about eight years old with the help of my provincial aunts and uncles who denounced me at every turn because I broke from the lifestyle that relegated southern Italians to a second-class status in this American society. That second-class status was pounded into my generation by our forbears and reinforced by the prejudices of American society throughout my youth and up to and including World War Two, when the United States and Italy declared war upon one another. When I volunteered for the Air Force, Army Intelligence and the F.B.I. subjected Grandpa and me to an exhaustive background check and put me through several psychological exams to ferret out any possible leaning on my behalf in favor of Italy.

Enough of that!

The book provides a good history of Italy going back to perhaps 400 B.C., but in greater detail from about 1200 A.D., when the Germans, Austrians, French and Spanish, along with Papal forces, ruled various areas in Italy.

Read it! You'll like it!

Love,

Your Papa

I pulled the book from the envelope: *Unto the Sons,* by Gay Talese—who, like my father, was the son of a tailor and seamstress, the first child of *Mezzogiorno* immigrants. Who, like my father, was born round the block from the Statue of Liberty, had grown up beneath her beacon and become a U.S. Air Force fan. Whose voice throughout the memoir was that of a whirling dervish pursuing spiritual ascent, through heart, through mind, beyond ego, in a quest for understanding, towards forgiveness, love and truth.

In his book, Talese writes that as the son of Italians he always felt himself an outsider, different from his boyhood friends in almost every way—the clothes he wore, the food in his lunch pail, the music his family played. He says he felt unrelated even to his parents, especially his father, who actually was a foreigner who spoke accented English. He recalls seeing letters for his father arrive bearing strange stamps and sometimes enclosing photographs of oddly-uniformed men. He remembers his father explaining that the men were his uncles and cousins; they were in the Italian army and fighting the United States.

I paused as I read this confession—for the voice I heard was not Talese's, but my father's as he never spoke. My father, self-possessed, arrogant; could it be that he lacked confidence? My father, prejudiced, tactless; had he been scoffed, misunderstood? My father, who I'd never pleased; had he been disparaged by his parents? The man I wanted to applaud me—did he long for approval too? These were questions I'd never thought to ask. Still, the last scene of *Unto the Sons* seemed my father's response.

There, ten-year-old Gay sits in the kitchen with a bowl of cereal. He's reading the newspaper headlines, looking at the photos on the front page: smoke rising from Monte Cassino, an Italian cloister for Benedictine monks who'd lived there for fourteen centuries, until the Nazis seized it and moved in. He learns that American B-17s have razed it with kilotons of bombs.

After breakfast, Gay hears cursing and pounding on the walls of his house. He opens his bedroom door, sees his father, in overcoat and hat, swatting the model airplanes hung there from ceiling threads. They are American bombers, balsa-framed, paper-covered, painted, and Gay has spent years crafting them; they're the proudest achievements of his life. "Stop it, they're mine!" he screams. But his father keeps swinging both hands till he's knocked down all the airplanes and smashed them to smithereens.

Talese's father, my father's father, mine—who'd forsaken their fathers for their children. Who'd toiled and struggled so their children could live more easily than they. Whose children's success—sacrifice-purchased—wound up pricking them with envy, never sufficing because it wasn't theirs. Whose words and actions seemed censure to their children, but were really expressions of grief—grief for themselves—snarled with faith that their children would fly.

And now my father was dying. Did he know I loved him too?

My father was in a coma when I arrived at Saint Lucie Medical Center. He lay in critical care, ashen beneath a sheet, feet poking out. A tube had been plunged down his throat, his body a catheter maze surrounded by whooshing machines. I threaded my way through a knot of nurses, took my father's hand. "Dad?"

Fluttering eyelids, the only response.

My father died ten days later in the middle of the night, never having regained consciousness. I cried alone in the dark of my mother's great room, hunched over my knees.

Outside, a sudden humming drone. Drying my eyes with my shirtsleeve, I looked up through the skylight. In the moon's halo, an airplane was rising, dipping its wings, blinking white lights.

Seeds on the Wind

September 1989

I stepped into the prism of sunshine that illuminated the tiny bathroom. Steam rose around me, glistening in the light. Shaking mango-scented shower drops from my hair, I reached for my towel on its hook. I winced. There it was again, the cramp deep and low in my body, followed by the nauseating wave, then the tremulous unfurling of an inward peace. Thank you, God, for Cristin. And I pulled the towel tight around me, as if to hold her there.

"Mark," I'd said over dinner almost two years earlier. "I've been thinking. I just can't take my job anymore. Besides, I'm twenty-eight and we've been married four years. Maybe it's time to have a baby."

He glanced around our Murray Hill apartment—bedroom not much wider than a mattress, living room just large enough for a couch and table for two, kitchen, phone-booth big.

"A baby? Where would we put it?"

A quiver like a harp-string in my heart. "Well, at first we can keep her in our bedroom. I think a crib would fit next to your bike."

"Her?"

I looked into my plate, poked *farfalle* with my fork. "Or him. . ."

Though I'd already named her Cristin.

Cristin, an English-Latin name derived from the Greek χρίω, *chrio*, a translation of the Hebrew מָשִׁיחַ, *mashiyach*, messiah, savior. European variations—Christine, Kristen, Christiana—have been used since the Middle Ages, becoming trendy after the death of Saint Cristina.

The nuns who taught me Catechism in grade school often mentioned Saint Cristina, used her as a paragon of love. Born in

Italy in the third century, she was the only child of Urbino, a rich and powerful magistrate. Urbino was profoundly polytheistic, so he locked his daughter in a tower to shield her from Christianity and hand-picked her teachers.

Cristina loved to learn but hated the tower. Her only joy was walking, circling round the terrace, wondering at Creation. Moved by her meditations, God sent an angel to teach her The One True Faith. Then he set her free.

Cristina emerged from the tower a zealous Catholic. She smashed Urbino's idols and gave the gold fragments to the poor, prompting her father's rage. So he hung her from iron hooks, grilled her on white-hot coals, shot her with poison arrows. He hacked off her nubile breasts, cut out her prayerful tongue, assailed her with venomous snakes. He demanded she give up Christianity. But Cristina didn't die, wouldn't budge in her belief, and Urbino couldn't bear her insubordination. He tied her to a boulder, pitched her into Lake Bolsena.

Then an angel saved Cristina, and Urbino died of spite.

Cristin, divine without the A, was the substance of my daydreams. She'd be a spunky daughter, an infant savior. She'd release me from the bondage of my job, be a new beginning, a chance to do things right. She'd bring me complete fulfillment and unconditional love.

But only if Mark agreed. Silent, he stood up from the table, stacked dishes, disappeared into the kitchen. Gushing water, banging cupboards, clanging pots.

Hands clasped upon the placemat, I sat alone, circling my thumbs.

"All right," he called out. "If that's what you want."

So, we sprang to action: *Every morning / Every evening / Ain't we got fun? / Not much money / Oh but honey / Ain't we got fun?* And we did, at least at first. But pregnancy eluded me. We tried for six months without success.

• • • • •

My mother told me to try a basal thermometer, an ultra-sensitive thermometer that tracks the body's tiniest temperature shifts. It had worked for her when she had me. Each night, I should shake the thermometer down before going to bed and leave it on my nightstand. That way, I wouldn't have to move much to get it. Then, each morning, I should take my temperature first thing—always at the same exact time—and plot it on a chart. When I saw my temperature drop by 0.4 degrees, I would know I had ovulated and was fertile. Then I should have sex. The thermometer was easy to use, and, what's more, was recommended by the Church. I could even choose how to use it—orally, vaginally or rectally.

Jeez Mom, please.

My cousin Angela seconded the motion, but embellished: following sex, I should stand on my head. It had worked for her. After resting a moment, I should roll onto my stomach, slide my torso off the bed, leave my legs on the mattress forming a jackknife. I should rest my head between propped forearms on the floor. Gravity would help the sperm swim to the target egg. And beforehand, I shouldn't forget to vacuum under the bed with the hose attachment. This was very important as sneezing could disrupt the sperms' journey, throw them off course. She'd lost some months to dust.

Mark's sister Sue said she'd pray for me. She'd add me to the prayer tree at First Presbyterian. It was composed of practiced petitioners. Devoted, they got results.

So I bought a basal thermometer, swept beneath the bed, prayed God would answer the prayer-tree's prayers and continued to dream about Cristin. She'd be blue-eyed like Mark, dark-haired like my mother, beautiful as I'd never been. Bighearted as Sue and Angela, playful as my grandfather, bold as I wished I could be. Assiduous like Mark's father, brilliant like mine, reflective like me.

I imagined her as a baby in a reclining bouncer seat, chewing on the frog jelly teether, batting the donut rattle. She'd pump her legs with Mark's athletic power, jab the toys with my curiosity.

I saw her as a toddler on the floor with her Lego Town set, stacking reds and yellows to make a house, linking the greens to construct a lawn. She'd choose the right blocks with Mark's geometric prowess, make it lovely with my creativity.

I pictured her as a schoolgirl in a pleated plaid skirt, reading *Charlotte's Web*, collecting autumn leaves. She'd recite the presidents' names with Mark's precision, eagerly raise her hand in class like the pre-law-school me.

I envisioned her as a teenager. She would flash her blue eyes when she came home from high school, flick her chestnut hair, say "Mom. I got my paper back. " Smiling, she'd hand me the paper, *98%* emblazoned at the top. I would read her teacher's comments one by one: "Nice!" "Interesting!" "Insightful!" Then I'd say, "Honey, great job!" and give my girl a hug.

Cristin. I'd extol every eyelash she fluttered, praise every tiny triumph of her life.

After eight months, I went to see Dr. Kapoor. Sitting behind her desk in a turquoise sari, she flipped through my file, then smoothed her sleek black hair into a tight chignon. "So, you are here for infertility."

I noted the vermilion *bindi* on her forehead, knew it expressed a wife's wish for her husband's long life. I wondered if she had children.

Over the course of the next few months, I often focused my eyes on her *bindi*, gritting my teeth. In July, when she tourniquetted my bicep, needled my elbow crook vein and siphoned blood to fill a rack of vials. In August, when she lay me full-bladdered on the table ("Please hold"), slid the cold transducer in my vagina and prodded it to view my uterus on the screen. In September, when she stirruped my feet, threaded the catheter through my cervix, filled my womb with warm contrast fluid and clicked a series of X-rays. In October, when she seated me knees-pressed-to-shoulders, jabbed a thin rod through my os, scraped my uterine lining ("Do you feel discomfort?") and placed the tissue in a jar. Dr. Kapoor's forehead, a *bindi*-brace against pain.

In November, Dr. Kapoor confirmed the tests results. She could find no fertility problem with either me or Mark (who'd spent some moments in a private room with a jar and *Playboy*). "Relax. And give it more time."

But the months kept slipping away: December, January, February, March, April—each a cycle of emotions just like the one before:

Day 1-6, pre-fertile days:	"This month it will happen!"
Days 7-11, fertile days:	"Let's do it, do it, do it.
Days 12-16, waiting days:	"I feel a bit strange. Can it be?"
Days 17-23, countdown days:	"Oh, I know, I know, this is it!
Days 24-30, menstrual days:	"God, I don't want to live."

Why can't I make a baby? Even rats and donkeys can do that.

Dr. Kapoor prescribed Clomid, said it would augment my fertility by prompting robust ovulation. Beginning on the third day of full-flow menstruation, I should take one pill each morning for five consecutive days. Possible side effects were few: enlargement of the ovaries, hot flashes, abdominal pain or bloating, nausea or vomiting, breast pain, headache, abnormal menstrual bleeding. So I sweated, swelled, threw up, throbbed throughout May. And I pictured Cristin on her wedding day—tall as Mark's sister, slender as my cousin, she would descend the spiral staircase of our Tudor, smiling in my lace gown and my mother's pearls.

• • • • •

June, day 30. Tossing my bath towel on the bed, I slipped into my undergarments, examined my belly in the mirror. I was six days late, meaning Cristin was three weeks old. From the shelf above the desk I pulled out *Behold Man,* a gift from my college boyfriend Dave. I flipped to "Early Fetal Development," found her picture on page 53. She looked like a lucent pink chameleon, umbilical blood suffusing crimson heart. I smiled at her white leg knob, the flipper of her arm. I admired her curving-ladder spine, the faint dimple of her eye.

Another cramp and flutter. God, thank you for Cristin. The next morning I'd take the pregnancy test I'd hidden in the bathroom. I'd collect my morning urine in the cup, pipette a drop to the reagent. Placing the test tube in the mirrored holder, I'd watch the colored ring gather, reflect. Then I'd burst into the bedroom with the evidence, exhibit it to Mark.

But by late morning, I feared I wasn't pregnant—retching gut, pulsing womb, piercing pain. I hurried from my office to the bathroom, locked myself in a stall. When I saw the scarlet flag, I doubled over and cried: What am I doing in the *Women's* Room? I'm not even female.

Slipping into the hallway, I hurried past the offices of my colleagues, rushed down the elevator, through the building lobby, head bowed to hide my tears.

I emerged from the building on 42nd Street—brilliant sky, pink-budded trees. People swarmed the noontime sidewalks. Kids strutted with Walkmans, businessmen loosened ties, couples held hands laughing, vendors shouted, "Getcha hot dawgs, heya!" Mothers pushed Gracos by shop windows, babies' faces bright midday moons. In Manhattan, life surged everywhere except inside of me.

On 50ᵗʰ Street, I ducked into Saint Patrick's, chill church air drying my cheeks. Sliding into a pew, I looked about the nave—the High Altar's lacy *baldacchino*, the *lierne* ceiling vaulted with stars. Sunlit stained glass windows cast kaleidoscopes on my hands and knees. I studied the Annunciation window—Gabriel tendering a lily, emerald tunic, pearly wings. Mary turning from her needlework, topaz halo, ruby shawl. God with his citrine nimbus releasing a dove from a cloud. I locked his eyes with my gaze: Why won't you send me a baby?

Silence.

What a fool I am.

The next morning I awoke in bed, window sun warm on my cheeks. I got up to look out. On a terrace of a neighboring building, a man clipped flowers from a tall potted rose. He drew pink blossoms to his nose, lingered, tipped water from a can.

"Mark," I said at breakfast, staring in my coffee cup. "Dr. Kapoor says I should relax. Maybe we should move from New York, find a less stressful place to live."

Seattle, Washington. *The Rand McNally Places Rated Guide* had ranked it fourth best city in the country, based on eleven parameters: housing (cheap), transportation (good), environment (clean). Health care (great), education (good), economics (strong). Climate (temperate), the arts (good), violent crime (low). Recreation (great), terrain (magnificent).

So we followed Horace Greeley's advice: "Go West, young man and grow with the country!" But I hoped the growth would be the wife's. In Seattle, we both found law firm jobs: Mark's a plum to begin saving money, mine part-time to ease the stress. We bought a tiny house with a yard. I planted a little garden. And after a few more red flags, I called Dr. Swift.

•   •   •   •   •

Dr. Swift was a renowned specialist at the Seattle Infertility Clinic. His brochure included testimonials accompanied by family photos. In one, a young couple smiled with a moonfaced babe in arms, the family's blue eyes twinkling: "You'll see, Dr. Swift works wonders. He gave us our Gracey!"

Dr. Swift said Dr. Kapoor had done everything right. We'd continue the Clomid she'd prescribed, but ramp it up a notch. Every other day I would come into his office. On pill day 3, his nurse Sarah would do a blood test to assess my hormone levels; at each visit, she'd ultrasound my ovaries to measure follicle size. When one reached eighteen millimeters, she'd give me an H.C.G. injection to trigger ovulation. She would call in Mark soon afterwards. He'd produce a semen sample (*Playboy* plus jar again), which the clinic would wash and centrifuge, siphoning off the deadbeat sperm, assembling the Matt Biondis. Then Sarah would insert a catheter into my uterus, inject the sperm. "Soon," Dr. Swift said, "you'll see your child's heartbeat on the ultrasound."

Six months of sex with a syringe (Sarah, presenting the labeled vial: "Please confirm this is your husband!" Me, stirrupped, semi-nudely nodding, "Yes, yes, that's him!"). But I never saw our baby's heartbeat, just more scarlet flags.

One May day, I went out to our garden in tears. Rhododendrons bloomed fuchsia, coral. White clematis dangled from a tree. I breathed in the sweet spring fragrance. Wiping my cheeks with my sleeve, I spotted some campanulas lazing with my daylilies. Delicate bell-shaped flowers, violet cups of sun. But I'd never planted campanulas.

Maybe a seasoned gardener wouldn't have marveled at some stray flowers. But I never expected seeds from elsewhere, scattered by butterflies and wind, would sow themselves in my bed, presume adoption by me.

• • • • •

Naturally, I'd thought about adoption during my three years of infertility. But adoption meant I'd never know the life-pulse of a baby deep inside me, my child's prenatal dance. Or feel the private deluge or shout, "Mark, I think it's time!" Or push to his rhythmic coxswaining as our baby sculled into this world. Or drowse with our baby at my breast.

Besides, I'd heard dozens of couples competed for every healthy infant, that only the superrich succeeded, especially those who owned horses. We had a tiny house. We didn't even own a cat. So what kind of baby could we get? What if our baby was the child of an AIDs or drug-addicted mother? What if our baby was handicapped? Or wasn't cute or smart? And how would it be to have a baby who wasn't Caucasian like us? I'd read of people who called cross-race adoption ethnic genocide. They scorned the melting pot. They disdained assimilation. Would they be hostile to us? Would they ridicule our child? And would our parents accept a black baby or a child from India or China? Could Mark and I?

Sometimes the thought of adoption kicked my heart like a donkey's hind legs. Other times I chastised myself for being pigheaded, narcissistic, prejudiced. Who was I to balk when there were babies needing homes? And, oh, those violet campanulas, as lovely in our garden as any flower I'd planted myself.

We applied to the India program of the A.F.C. adoption agency. We filled out myriad forms, visited adoptive homes. We went through a series of interviews ("Yes, we'll send the child to college. Sorry, we don't own a horse."), escorted social workers through our home ("Of course I clean under the bed."), scheduled the doctor exams. And we papered the tiny spare bedroom—teddy bears bobbing blue and pink balloons.

I was stirring soup for dinner when Mark came from his physical. He laid his briefcase on the table. I turned from the stove. "So, how'd it go?"

"Dr. Morris felt a pea-sized lump on my testicle. He said it's probably nothing, but did a biopsy."

The diagnosis: testicular cancer, the most common cancer in thirty-something men. Dr. Morris scheduled surgery that week. He'd remove Mark's testicle, then treat him with radiation.

When the surgeons were through operating, a nurse escorted me to Mark. He lay on a wheeled narrow bed, sheet pulled up to his chin. His hands and feet protruded, marked with purple stigmata, diagnostic dye injection sites.

I took his hand, head throbbing like a wound: Now I'll never be pregnant. But if I had been, we would have missed the tumor, and Mark would have died. Thank God, Mark had the exam. Mark, I love you, wake up. But what will A.F.C. say? Please God, let Mark live.

I looked up at the nurse. She didn't have a *bindi*.

I received the letter from A.F.C. when Mark was back at work. They'd suspend our application till Mark had been cancer-free five years, till both of us were thirty-six.

Sometimes I still wonder at that moment. I stared at the letter dry-eyed, crumpled it, threw it on the floor. Not knowing where I was going, I climbed into my car and drove. Finding myself at the library, I unshelved a physician directory, made an obstetrician list and wrote:

Dear Doctor:

We are seeking to adopt an infant through a private placement. We would greatly appreciate your recommending us to anyone you know who may wish to place an infant now or in the future. Please feel free to share the following information (except for our last name and address) and the enclosed photograph with anyone who may be interested.

Our names are Mark and Jan. Mark was born in Chicago, and

Jan was born in New York. Both of us were raised in the suburbs of New York City, where most of our family still live. We met each other when we were seniors at Bucknell University in Pennsylvania and married two years later. We've been married seven years.

We have no children, although we have been trying to have one for three years. Since having a family is important to us, we decided to build one through adoption.

We believe we will be good parents for our adopted child. Our marriage is a strong and happy one, and we can offer our child a stable, loving home. We own our own house and are financially secure. Both of us are attorneys. Although we are very different from each other, we complement each other well.

Mark is quiet, somewhat reserved, but thoughtful and affectionate. His favorite activity is cycling, and he has done tours in several states. He also enjoys skiing, running, weight lifting, photography and reading. He is tall, with dark blond hair and blue eyes.

Jan is gregarious, emotional and loving. She likes to work out, and especially enjoys aerobics. She loves doing art work, gardening and reading. She is not crazy about practicing law, and looks forward to being a full-time mother. Jan is petite, with brown hair and eyes.

We would love to share our selves, home, activities, friends and family with a child. We have no preferences with respect to a child, except that he or she be healthy. We hope that one day you will contact us about an adoption.

I mailed the letter and snapshot to fifty doctors in three states. Even now I keep a copy of the photo on the table in our hall. Mark and I standing in our garden, arms around each other's waist, he in a gray suit and tie, me in a skirt and violet blouse. We are young, smiling and trim, backed by a green burst of maple leaves, the picture frame purple like my blouse.

• • • • •

One afternoon that summer, I was digging in the garden, striking my shovel through the soil, stomping on the blade. A dozen antique roses waited for planting, yellow, white and pink, apple-scented in the heat.

The telephone rang inside the kitchen. Dirty palm wiping sweaty forehead, leaning on my shovel shaft, I hoped it would stop. It persisted. Damn. I tramped inside.

"Jan?" Mark's voice, taut. "A doctor from Bellingham just called. Last night a teenage girl had a baby she wants someone to adopt. The baby's premature. Her weight is only five pounds and there's a problem with her colon. I don't remember what it's called. The mother smoked while pregnant and had no prenatal care."

When I still hoped for pregnancy, I'd read *What to Expect When You're Expecting*. I clearly recalled the warning: "Stop smoking. No ifs, ands or butts." Smoking nearly doubles the odds of low-weight, prematurity, birth defects and mental retardation.

"Jan," Mark said. "What do you think we ought to do?"

But I couldn't speak. Tears fell onto my wrists as I scraped dirt from under my nails.

We drove to Saint Gianna's Hospital, rode the elevator silent, holding hands. Emerging at the nursery, an expanse of finger-printed glass, we peered at the row of bassinettes, but there were no babies inside. My heart, a bloodless fist.

Was it despair or relief? Because I wanted to be a mother. But this child's prospects for thriving were doubtful, far less than the best. Yet somehow she'd come to me and Mark. Was her coming to us serendipitous, or was she somehow meant to be ours? Wasn't my mothering motive a desire to give love I never felt? Unconditional love, precisely the kind this child needed. Would I be able to give it? Or discover I was just like my dad?

"Mark, maybe we should leave."

Inside the room a nurse stood before a window, her back to us. Mark nudged me toward the threshold. "Let's go in and ask."

We stepped in the prism of sunshine that illuminated the nursery. The woman turned around. She was cradling a sleeping newborn. "Oh, you must be Mark and Jan." Smiling, she held the baby out towards me, settled her in my arms.

Tightly swaddled, pink blanket to nose, knit cap to brow, tiny as a doll.

The nurse reached over the baby, gently stroked her cheek. "Since she's premature, we need to keep her warm." She inched off the baby's cap, pushed the blanket from her face.

I held her close to my heart. Cristin yawned, opened honey eyes.

Two years later, I stood in an operating room wearing surgical scrubs. Hospital rules provided only one family member could be present. Nurses buzzed around, readying forceps and scalpels. An anesthesiologist worked the I.V., checked the electrocardiograph.

I looked at the woman on the table. Freckles across her nose, eyes closed, breathing slow and steady. Her bare belly bulged from a sea of deep blue cloth. She'd wanted me to be present and to be unconscious herself.

Mark and I had met her twice. Young, unemployed, unmarried, five months pregnant, she'd wandered into the doctor's, asked for a check-up and adoption advice. He'd pulled our old letter from a file, where it had been since before Cristin's birth. She chose us because I was Catholic and our first names were Jan and Janet. And so our son would be Sean, an Irish variation of the Hebrew וחנן, Yochanan, John. It means God is gracious, the masculine form of Jan.

The obstetrician came into the room, holding out freshly-scrubbed forearms and hands. He chose a scalpel from a tray as the nurses gathered round. Poising its tip below his patient's navel, he nodded at his assistants. A quick slash, a glint of steel. A swarm of elbows and hands like bees around a hive. Then a bloody eel slithering from the wound, draped between the table and the doctor's hands.

The doctor fussed a bit. Then he looked at me. "Jan, I need your help." He motioned to a tray with his elbow. "You'll need the scissors and the clamp."

Moving beside the doctor, I took the instruments from the tray, slipped the scissors on my fingers—flashing vision of a long ago cadaver and squirming fetal rats. How odd to think that when I lived on the East Coast, my children's ova were three thousand miles away. Then I pictured Cristin—ponytail on the top of her head spurting a fountain of curls, playing "So Big" with Mark, bouncing to the Beach Boys' "Kokomo." Her colon had been corrected. But would she have other health issues, become a good student, have interests like ours? Would her baby cuteness mature to teenage beauty? I didn't know, just like any other parent.

So I turned to Sean—his slimy, bloodied body, his writhing head and limbs. I spread the scissor blades apart, cut and clamped the cord, as his eyes flickered green.

Ground Zero

*T*he atrium of the Century Square Building was silent that Monday morning. Gray marble, black crystal-veined, echoed beneath my footsteps, embraced the chill air around me, rose, its smooth massive slabs supporting the glass dome above. I looked up as I once had at the *Basilica di San Pietro*. But God's frescoed hand didn't reach from the rafters to bless me. His gilded words didn't call from the stone to dispel my doubts: *TV ES PETRVS ET SVPER HANC PETRAM AEDIFICABO ECCLESIAM MEAM; TIBI DABO CLAVES REGNI CAELORVM*—YOU ARE ROCK AND ON THIS ROCK I WILL BUILD MY CHURCH; TO YOU I WILL GIVE THE KEYS TO THE KINGDOM OF HEAVEN. Instead, beyond the panes, only dark nimbostratus clouds.

The elevator doors slid open. I passed through them, pressed twenty-six, was sealed alone in the maple box ascending, counting the beeps to my floor. Emerging to an airy vestibule, I nodded at the receptionist: "Morning, Laurie," eyed the proclamation etched in glass: Turnbull Brewster Dickson, Attorneys at Law. Turning down a hallway carpeted in ecru Berber and paneled in cherry-wood, I slipped by the offices of my colleagues, some braying on speakerphones ("No, that's *pa*tently unacceptable!"), others keying on flat-screen computers (tkk-tkk-tkk-tkk-tkk), several droning into hand-held Dictaphones ("In consideration of the respective agreements herein set forth..."). I moved down the corridor swiftly, barely conscious of the spot-lit modern art—an Imogen Cunningham silver print magnolia blossom; a Mark Tobey casein on paper, squiggly tongues of flame—or the brass door plaque inscribed with my name.

Polished stone, sparkling glass, fine waxed wood, gleaming brass—all to assure the public, our clients, ourselves: We are distinguished, sophisticated, refined—foundations of civilization. Soft carpet, sleek gadgets, custom lighting, tony art—all testimonials to our character: We are innovative, prosperous, cultured—guardians of humanity.

Entering my twelve-by-twelve office, I flung my briefcase in a corner, settled in my ergonomic chair, gazed out the large picture window at Seattle—north over the Bon Marché rooftop, mechanical systems, ever-whirling gears. Out toward the burnished Space Needle, flying saucer tethered to a field. West above huddled Pike Place Market, flickering neon sign red on the horizon. Out toward steely Puget Sound girded by white Olympic peaks.

Oh, what a view. That's what life was about. More than construction materials, a view was the barometer of merit, the symbolic revelation of success—view as rated by region: South (+0), Midwest (+1), Pacific Northwest (+2), California (+3), Northeast (+4), Manhattan (+5). View as appraised by focal point: eyesore (-1), building wall (+0), cityscape (+1), landmark (+2), mountains (+3), ocean (+4). View as valued by height: low (+0), medium (+3), high (+5).

Seen that way, some might say I'd already declined in my eighteen years as lawyer. Although my vista was lovely (+14), second only to higher-up west views (+17), it couldn't compare to the panorama I'd enjoyed in New York when young (+28).

In my first years out of law school, I looked out from double-hung neo-Gothic windows near the top of the Lincoln Building (floor forty-eight) in midtown Manhattan—south beyond myriad landmarks—the Empire State Building, Grace Church, Brooklyn Bridge. Out to the Statue of Liberty walking sequined waters in the sun. Down to the Twin Towers, armor-clad Goliaths keeping watch.

The Twin Towers. One-hundred-ten stories each, home to gargantuan businesses—Morgan Stanley, Cantor Fitzgerald, Port Authority—topped by Windows on the World (for starters: terrine of *foie gras, mesclun* in truffle oil: $35.00). Who could have ever imagined the images they'd come to conjure? An airplane piercing each tower like a rapier to the neck. The double explosions, amber infernos, black smoke wreaths against the blue. People leaping from windows, some solo, others holding hands—fathers, mothers, sons, daughters, relatives, lovers, colleagues and friends. Paired pillars of steel, pulverized to powder, suspended like a specter for a moment, then sinking, snowing ash. And who will ever forget the world's bewildered babble?

DODS-ZONE!

ATTACCO ALLA CIVILTÀ!

DIE WELT UNTER SHOCK!

התקפה על העולם

TERROR ATTACKS!

PANICO MUNDIAL!

「世界の攻撃

O ATENTADO QUE MUDOU O MUNDO!

DIS OORLOG!

I will never forget. I saw the Twin Towers crumble on the Seattle morning news while I was ironing the blouse I'd wear to the office that day. Ever since, I couldn't focus on my work.

Really, even in the best times, my work was difficult for me. Law hadn't inspired me in law school and grew more wearisome with the years—sitting at my desk reworking stilted pre-fabricated contracts, frenzied to meet a deadline the client would later postpone. Billing time that never slaked the partners, sacrificing weekends, nights and holidays to the cause. Spending hours in conference rooms negotiating monumental minutiae, straining to maintain goodwill between cantankerous landlords and tenants. Often during meetings, part of my mind would detach from my brain, rise and hover in a corner, listen to words streaming from my mouth—"How about one-third of the T.I. allowance payable upon full signature by the parties, one-third upon landlord's inspection and approval of the finish work to take place no later than ten days prior to the scheduled commencement date, and the balance upon the actual commencement date, provided that tenant has opened for business in the premises; otherwise, on the date tenant first opens for business?" Then I'd hear an inner voice admonish: What on earth? What the hell?

The hell was this: I'd wanted to quit my job for years but could never gather the gumption to give up the coveted goods: stability, affluence, prestige. To press the elevator button, take the ride in descent, trade the view for the ground—a trade two thousand Tower victims never had the chance to make.

As I stared out my office window, a ferry drifted into sight, docked at Pier 52. Later, I knew, it would change direction, depart Seattle for Bainbridge, fore becoming aft. How I wished I could do the same.

In those days, I often had a dream, sometimes still do. I'm in a house, climbing stairs, walking hallways. Rarely, it's modern, picture windowed; more often Tudor, dark beamed with leaded panes. Its halls are lined with doors knobbed in iron, pewter, glass. I choose a brass knob like a flower, enter a chamber with deep violet walls. Window light filters through an oak tree casting shifting shadows upon another door. I open to a second room, rose red, then another, another, another— green, saffron, flax blue—a Russian Babushka doll of rooms, my heart, a hummingbird.

I stand before another door, a crystal knob. Should I turn it—or turn back?

I twist the knob, open the door—golden light from an arched

leaded window rebounds from a mirrored armoire. I squint my eyes, pull the armoire doors; my reflection flickers at me, and I find myself in a chamber, walls studded with infinite hooks, each hung with dresses. Frenzied, I pluck the dresses, eye them one by one—baby doll, fuchsia, flapper, lilac; caftan, periwinkle, toga, pink—I toss them, May Day petals—not this one, not this one or this. Then a sheath, silky in my fingers. I hug it to my body, sense a perfect fit. But the light eclipses from the window. In darkness, I wake up.

My father had always assured me, as a lawyer I could do anything. Some lawyers had left my firm to work at Starbucks, Amazon, Google. Others had left to teach tax at the U.W. School of Law. But none of those situations called to me. Only Mr. Kohler did.

Mr. Kohler taught tenth-grade English at Baldwin Senior High. Dark hair flopping in his eyes, spirited as a sprite, his sugarplum lips spouted Shakespeare: "If you can look into the seeds of time / and say which grain will grow and which will not, / speak then unto me."

For you, Mr. Kohler, anything.

The competition was stiff, though. Dori Klein had wavy chestnut hair, enormous indigo eyes. Karen Wilde knew how to spell renaissance with two s's and only one n. Wendy Levine spewed wacky jokes: "What did the pencil say to the paper?. . .I dot my eye on you!"

Still, Mr. Kohler penned a graceful *A* on everything I wrote—my *David Copperfield* paper, my peace essay, my seagull poem. And when he started a drama club, he took me by the elbow. "If you can write, you can act!"

I glanced at Dori Klein. "No, I really can't."

"Nonsense! We'll meet at three o'clock."

On the night of the *Shakespearean Revue* all was atwitter backstage. My cousin Angela—hair and makeup—twirled me around to inspect her work: my hair parted in the middle, a ribbon running through a braid, my gown of beaded lemon yellow, its crinolines rustling as I moved.

Still, my stomach roiled. Earlier, I had begged my mother, "Please remember to clap!" She hugged me, kissed my forehead and vanished in the crowd.

Suddenly all was quiet, and Mr. Kohler winked and nodded. I moved to the blue X on the stage in the velvet-curtained darkness: Please God, let me be good.

Pulleys whirring, curtains lurching, dust clouds wisped across the stage. Theater midnight, click, a spotlight star. I looked up and spoke to it:

"O Romeo, Romeo! Wherefore art thou Romeo?

Deny thy father, and refuse thy name;

Or, if thou wilt not, be but sworn my love,

And I'll no longer be a Capulet.

What's in a name? That which we call a rose

By any other name would smell as sweet;

So Romeo would, were he not Romeo call'd,

Retain that dear perfection which he owes

Without that title."

Click, darkness, whirring curtains. I felt giddy and light. But no Romeo rose from the shadows; no applause broke the silence of the night.

I rushed, crying, to the wings, Mr. Kohler catching me. I was choking on my mucous. "No one clapped for me!"

He raised my chin with a finger as I blinked back my tears. "Would you clap if an angel sang in church?"

Oh, the power of a teacher.

Later I learned from my own children, a teacher's power can also be perilous. Take the Tuesday I returned to my office after meeting with clients. Sitting at my desk, I speakered the voicemails I'd received, finger impatient on the *skip*, heart rate tripling with each beep:

12:47 p.m.: "Mrs. Vallone. This is Mr. Rogers, principal of Cascade Elementary. Mrs. Dixon has just reported Sean missing from the second-grade classroom. We're in the process of searching the wing and will call you as soon as we know something. No need to be alar—"

1: 18 p.m.: "Mrs. Vallone—Mr. Rogers again. We've searched both the building and playground and haven't found Sean. The police have been notified. We haven't been able to reach your hus—"

1: 52 p.m.: "Mrs. Vallone—Hello, Rogers. We've just received a call from the police. They've patrolled the local streets, but no sign—"

2:05 p.m.: "Mrs. Vallone—good news. We have Sean. He rang the doorbell of a house about two miles up the road. The woman called the police. Sean will be with me for the remainder of the day. Please come in when you pick him up."

I met with Mr. Rogers after school, Sean leaping on my lap as soon as I took a seat. Mr. Rogers—Izod, Dockers, Sperrys—swiveled into his chair, straightened some papers on his desk, stretched a smile at my seven-year-old. "How about telling your mom what happened, and then you can take a treat." He motioned to a gum machine standing in a corner, glass globe chock-a-block with rainbow balls.

Sean wriggled off my knees to face me, his back to Mr. Rogers. "Mrs. Dixon gave back our math homework, but I didn't get mine. So I asked her if she had it. She said maybe it was the one missing a name. So I looked and it was. But then Kayla said it was hers and Mrs. Dixon looked and said it was too neat to be a boy's. But I told her it was mine. And she called me a liar and gave it to Kayla. So I said I wasn't. So she said it again. Liar! Liar!" His voice had risen an octave. "Mommy, it was mine! So a little later I asked to go to the bathroom and she said okay. And I sneaked out and started walking home. But I got lost, so I went to a house and the lady called the police. The car was cool. They let me hear the siren." Sean turned, reached a palm to Mr. Rogers, who gave him a penny for gum.

Mr. Rogers smiled again. "Sean's made some poor choices today. Mrs. Dixon assures me the homework is Kayla's."

Mindy Lippshitz. A name, three decades buried, instantly disinterred. In sixth grade she'd been assigned my project partner. Over a weekend, we were to build a model igloo, but she didn't show up for our work date. Dinner knife as my blade, Elmer's for mortar, I spent Sunday after Mass shave-and-gluing till I'd formed a sugar cube dome Michelangelo would have admired. Monday morning at school, I set it on the display among tepees, log cabins, adobes, yurts, sod houses, thatched huts. When Mindy saw the igloo, she swooped it off the table: "Mrs. Zenowitz, look how good ours is!"

I tugged Sean back on my lap. "Mr. Rogers, you need to understand. Running away from school is not a *choice*—it's *forbidden*! So is calling a child a liar, especially without proof."

A year later, Cristin was the dupe. One month into the school year, her fifth grade teacher called and asked me in to see her. When I knocked on her classroom door, Miss Bleaker turned from cleaning the blackboard, placed the eraser on the rest, rap-slapped her hands wafting chalk dust. "Oh hello, Mrs. Vallone. Please have a seat." Pointing at a student desk, she handed me a sheet of paper, sat at her big desk.

I squeezed into the low first row seat, smiled up at Miss Bleaker— her black banged-and-bobbed hair, her pink floppy-tie blouse. Then I looked down at the sheet:

Jamestown Quiz

Teacher: Miss Bleaker   Student: *Cristin*

Directions: Read each question carefully and circle the correct answer.

1. By 1620, Jamestown had become a more diverse colony due to the arrival of: ✗

    (a) African men and women

    b) women and Africans

    c) women and children

2. The arrival of Africans in Jamestown would make it possible to: ✗

    (a) grow more food

    b) expand the tobacco economy

    c) plant more corn

3. Many changes took place to help the early settlers of Jamestown survive. Which was NOT one of those changes? ✗

    a) Two ships arrived bringing needed supplies.

    b) Captain John Smith became a strong leader.

    (c) Slaves arrived from Africa and took over farming duties.

My head whirring, letters blurring. Women, children, Africans. Ships, captain, slaves. I looked up at Miss Bleaker.

She leaned forward, crossing forearms on the desk. "When a student fails this early in the year, it's my practice to meet with the parents. I'm concerned about Cristin. I suspect a learning disability."

My mind, suddenly sharp. "Based upon one quiz? Cristin did fine in fourth grade."

She pushed back in her seat. "She needs professional testing."

I remembered myself a first grader, the phonics quiz Mrs. Hanes gave, the sketches, one labeled *log*. We were to choose from among three others—*ball, lake, dog*—the one that rhymed with the first, *all* or *none*. Mrs. Hanes marked my *none* wrong and I didn't get my *100*. My father was perplexed when he saw it (puff, puff: "The teacher's a *mamaluke*.").

My mother called Mrs. Hanes: "Maybe in Buffalo *lahg* and *dawg* rhyme, but on Lawnguylind they don't." Still, the grade remained.

I pointed at Cristin's test. "Miss Bleaker, these questions—they're ambiguous. The first one, for ex—"

"I'm sorry, Mrs. Vallone. The truth is, there are some children who are not college material. It's best to accept that now. But proper help might get Cristin through high school."

"She's ten!"

She stood, tugged taut her pants suit jacket. "The school counselor can recommend a psychiatrist to perform the diagnostic test."

I thanked her, walked out of the classroom.

I didn't know at the time, that Cristin would struggle through fifth grade. Through sixth, seventh, eighth, ninth through twelfth. Despite special study skills courses. Despite seeing tutors after school. Despite the hours we prepped for exams. Thinking myself progressive, before becoming a parent, I'd vowed to praise my future children's Bs ("*88, Hon? Good job!*"), not imagining there existed kids like Cristin, who'd beaten me at Go Fish at age two, yet routinely earned Cs and Ds on tests.

And I didn't know at the time, that after applying to college, Cristin would dash daily to the mailbox as I locked the car from fetching her from school. Or that when the first slim envelope arrived, the one with the Breitlaken College logo, she would fling the pile of post across the pavement, papers fanning underneath the car, and charge into the house: "I knew it! A rejection!" Or that kneeling and groping for the letters, I'd discover Breitlaken's gone and hightail after my daughter. Or that I'd find her crumpled in a kitchen corner, face schoolmarm ink red, mascara-ed tears streaming, letter dangling from a hand. Or that she'd speak a name I'd thought seven years forgotten: "Miss Bleaker said I was stupid, but, look—I got in."

No, I didn't know these things as I walked out of Miss Bleaker's classroom. All I knew was Mr. Kohler would not confuse a quiz with a crystal ball, and that he—maybe even I—could write a better Jamestown quiz than that.

Esquire. At the age of forty-four, could I trade that title for teacher? Could I, like Juliet, deny my father, refuse the game? Could I be someone's Mr. Kohler? Of all my lawyer friends, only my neighbor Steve had left to teach kids. He'd quit law after just three years, become a history teacher at a tiny Jewish high school. One night I asked him about it, Miles Davis playing *Kind of Blue*.

"So Steve, I've been thinking of becoming an English teacher."

He set down his Chianti, lamplight through ruby stained glass. Nestling into the couch, he stroked his gray-flecked beard. "Didn't you major in science?"

"Biology, so what?" Piano vapor drifting, I curled my legs beneath me on the chair.

Steve cut a piece of brie, sucked ooze from his fingers. "It'd be tough. For the public schools, you'd need an English credential."

He popped the cheese in his mouth, flashed his eyebrows, chewed, as I felt myself morph into a panther pacing a cage to a trumpet riff.

"That's crazy. I'm a lawyer—a *professional* reader and writer!"

Steve shrugged, sipped his wine, two saxes snaking round the trumpet.

I choked on Steve's words for days. Why should I believe him? He worked at an oddball school. Clearly, he was out of touch. Hadn't I read a story about a national teacher shortage? About a fiftyish Manhattan judge who'd left the bench to teach high school in Harlem? I ransacked my stack of *Time* magazines, found the article I recalled. It said American colleges would graduate 200,000 new teachers that year, but school principals and reformers believed many would not be competent. So the states were recruiting professionals—seasoned doctors, accountants and lawyers—into fast-track teaching programs.

At work, I researched the law, discovered W.A.C. 180-82-334. It set the Washington requirements for entering English-teacher training programs: thirty semester credit hours in five subject areas:

1. The reading process (e.g., skills and strategies).
2. The writing process (e.g., expository, technical, narrative).
3. Communication (e.g., speaking, listening, and analyzing).
4. Language skills (conventions) and structure (social/historical).
5. Literature (e.g., American, British, world, and multicultural).

I photocopied the statute, brought it home with me. Then I found my old school transcripts and sat down to do the math:

Reading process	Legal Research / Analysis / Writing	2
Writing process	"	
Communication	Moot Court / Mock Trial	1
Language skills	Legal Research/ Analysis / Writing	
	German 1	4
	Italian 1 & 2	8
	Latin 1	4
Literature	Constitutional Law 1 & 2	8
	Philosophy / Religion / Drama 1 & 2	8
	German Literature in Translation	4
	German Literature 1 & 2	4
	Russian Culture	4
	American Literature I	4
	Chinese Literature in Translation	4

Total: 55. Almost double what I needed. So, Steve, take that! I called Seattle's schools of education and requested applications.

I was working at my desk—a Starbucks lease in New Jersey—when I answered the phone a few days later.

"Ms. Vallone? This is Dr. Oldham from the University of Washington."

I placed my pen on the blotter. My heart clenched; has Sean or Cristin been hurt at school? "Yes?"

Papers rustled on the line. "I have your application to the School of Education."

I rolled my eyes—oh one of *those* doctors (Ph. before the D.). "Dr. Oldham, thank you for calling. I didn't expect to hear so soon." I tilted my chair back from the kneehole, crossed ankles on desktop Mason-style. Clearly she was dying to have me. How many big firm lawyers could she get?

"I'm sorry, but we can't consider your application. You don't have sufficient English credits."

I dropped my feet to the floor. What, can't this woman add? "I have fifty-five credits. The statute requires only thirty."

"I count only seven."

"Seven?"

"That's right." She'd donned Nurse Ratched's voice. "There's no evidence on your transcripts that you've studied reading, expository or narrative writing, communication analysis, language skills, British or multicultural literature. We count two credits for technical writing, one for communication, four for American literature."

"Dr. Oldham, I'm a *lawyer*. Law's a combination of narrative and expository writing. Legal briefs *narrate* the facts, then *expose* precedents and law."

"Legal writing is technical."

"As for literature, I've studied dozens of novelists and playwrights— Brecht, Goethe, Hesse, Rilke, Aeschylus, Sophocles, Shakespeare—"

"I'm sorry; foreign writers must be in translation; you want to teach *English*. And course titles must exactly match the regulations, British Literature, World Literature and so on."

"Dr. Oldham. That's not how you read a statute!"

"I'm sorry." She hung up.

• • • • •

Years before I spoke with Dr. Oldham, I'd suspected my father had it wrong in thinking that lawyers could do anything. It began when Mark and I were looking for apartments in Manhattan. Each landlord we contacted required a rental application: name, address, job, employer, income, references. We'd turned in several applications, and each time were told a few days later the apartment had gone to someone else. Then we made a viewing appointment with a man who'd placed an ad to lease a one-bedroom in a Brownstone. After work, we started on our way—past Columbus Circle and up leafy Central Park West. We turned left on West 71st, found the house that matched the address, a tiny hydrangea garden surrounding the front steps. I turned to Mark, "I want to live here!"

We rang the Brownstone doorbell; the owner opened and stepped out. I told him I loved his flowers; he said that since his retirement he'd taken up gardening. Then he asked us what we did. Mark told him both of us were lawyers.

The man grew suddenly quiet, pinched off a wilting crimson flower cluster from a potted geranium. "I'm sorry, but we don't rent to lawyers."

Mark wrinkled his forehead. "Why not? We can pay the rent."

"Well, you know what they say—the difference between a lawyer and a catfish is that one's a bottom-dwelling scum sucker. The other is a fish."

So, I had long known that lawyers couldn't rent (Mark and I wound up buying a co-op) and it seemed, they couldn't teach either.

It's not that I really would have found the courage to leave my job. Investigating teaching was actually my third dalliance with quitting law. The first had been in year two when I was taking serigraphy at New York's School of Visual Arts. I loved the multi-step process—stretching silk taut over the wooden frame, stapling it round the edges. Blocking the screen with emulsion to form a hand-designed stencil (a negative of the image to be printed). Squeegeeing ink layers through the mesh and onto textured papyrus. Watching the colors form a painting through capillary action. Once, my instructor told me my sunset over the ocean—shades of cerulean and coral—showed potential. The next Monday I went to see Ralph Feldman, senior partner at Malkovich Fein. I gave him two weeks' notice I'd be leaving the firm to study art. Books packed in moving boxes, door plaque in my briefcase, I raced back to Ralph's office to withdraw my resignation on the last day.

My second attempt was in year nine when I was taking a garden design class at the U.W.'s Center for Urban Horticulture. To me there was nothing as glorious as digging dirt, making barren verdant, composing a chaos of flora bustling with butterflies and bees. I spent my weekends at the nursery buying snowdrops, bluebells, roses, monkshood, lilies, pinks, buddleias, hellebores and spiraeas, tilling them into the ground. When I ran out of space in my garden, sterile neighbor yards began to beckon, so I emailed Turnbull's managing partner that I'd be leaving to do landscape design. Within minutes she burst into my office: "Are you nuts?" Then she raised my pay.

Today I'm ashamed to admit it, but both times my thoughts and feelings were the same. Giving notice was the Boston Tea Party rushing towards the Fourth of July. Future, freedom, joy! But then my mind would turn to other parties, the kind I often went to with Mark. The kind that didn't serve tea, but martinis, *Merlot* and *chèvre chaud.* At these parties we'd meander through the crowd, toward a cluster of Mark's lawyer colleagues, and when we joined them Mark would say, "This is Jan, my wife." Then his friends would turn to me dull-eyed as they shook my hand. I always knew what they were thinking: she must be boring, idle, dumb. And I'd feel like a Roman candle, unlit, lying in the dirt. But with me working as a lawyer, Mark had always lit the fuse: "Jan's a lawyer too." Then his friends would turn to me, smiling. I'd become a pyrotechnic star shooting red and orange fire in the sky. So I just couldn't give up Mark's match.

Shortly after 9/11, I read Isabel Allende's short story "Little Heidelberg." At a tiny Caribbean dance hall, El Capitán, a retired Nordic sea captain, and Eloísa, a Russian chocolate maker, dance weekly for forty years, but they can't have a real conversation since he speaks only Nordic, she only Russian and Spanish. Then, one night at the Heidelberg, some Scandinavians arrive. El Capitán hears them speaking his language and asks them to translate his first words to Eloísa: "Will you marry me?"

Eloísa smiles. "Don't you think this is a little sudden? All right."

The couple begin to dance, whirling around the floor, one time, two times, three. They dance themselves into a frenzy, and as they do, Eloísa turns to lace. Another circle of the dance floor, and Eloísa turns to froth. Another, she becomes mist. Then El Capitán finds himself twirling round the dance floor empty-armed. All that's left of Eloísa is a lingering chocolate scent.

How I ached for El Capitán! For I whirled with a trace of silk screen ink mixed with stale hydrangea fragrance, while my birthplace New York City reeled with the stench of melted metal and bodies turned to ash.

Just as I'd foreseen, Seattle's ferry turned towards Bainbridge Island. As I watched it sally from the pier, sunlight splintered the clouds, the bay a cobalt-gray mosaic. I felt the tug of work, but really, there wasn't much to do. Ever since the Towers fell, mall stores had discontinued replication, hotels had halted new construction and office tenants high-rise relocation. But still, I had to bill my time, so when the telephone rang, I jumped and picked up my pen: "Turnbull Brewster Dickson."

"Hey, Jan. It's Steve calling from school."

I placed my pen back down.

"Jan, you probably won't believe it, but our English teacher starts maternity leave next week, and we're so disorganized, we still don't have a substitute. I hope you don't mind, but I mentioned you at this morning's staff meeting. The principal said he'd consider you. How about giving him a call?"

When I was confronting infertility, I often thought, Why me? I've always tried to be good; why do I deserve this? So I read a book I'd heard about, *When Bad Things Happen to Good People*, by Rabbi Harold Kushner, whose son had died at age fourteen. Kushner couldn't understand why the just God he believed in would allow a child to die—or the Holocaust to happen. After all, his son had been a good boy and Nazi victims innocent. He concluded God doesn't meddle or make or let things happen. Good and bad happen randomly to people—to people, good and bad. God's job is not to grant wishes, but to give people strength to live without.

After reading his book, I smiled politely when anybody told me everything happens for the best, is meant to be or is part of God's plan. What a silly, cruel delusion! I believed life is serendipity managed by choice if we're lucky. But when my children were born, I became unsure. I began to see that good had emerged from periods of bad. If Mark and I had not been infertile, we wouldn't have moved to Seattle, wouldn't have discovered his cancer, and Mark might have been dead. And we wouldn't have found Cristin and Sean and wouldn't have purchased our house. If we hadn't found Cristin and Sean, I wouldn't have learned to love children whose genetics aren't mine. If we hadn't purchased our house, I wouldn't have been friends with Steve. If I hadn't been friends with Steve, I wouldn't have received his call. If I hadn't discovered I love kids, I wouldn't have responded to it. And if

I hadn't responded to it, I would never have become a teacher. Was Steve's the call of God?

The Moshe Ben Maimon School is a yeshiva—an Orthodox Jewish high school. When it first opened in the seventies, its student body consisted of six boys and it convened in the basement of a building once a convent for Sacred Heart nuns. In the eighties some girls arrived. More sensitive to *feng shui* than their pioneering male counterparts, they complained about the space, calling it cramped and gloomy. So the school bought a building in the nineties, a clapboard former Baptist church, and fashioned it into seven classrooms, a small sanctuary cum library, a few rabbi offices, a lunchroom and an outdoor blacktopped basketball court. Five modular classrooms were added for the new millennium, when enrollment increased to ninety-five.

I was assigned to a classroom on the ground floor of the main building, where I'd spend a six-week leave from Turnbull, whose partners seemed pleased, given the business slump, to divert my finger from the pie. Maybe I would love teaching. If I did, I would leave Turnbull; if I didn't, I would go back.

I surveyed the tiny classroom—a dented metal teacher desk with locked drawers missing their key. A Neanderthal P.C. sans mouse, a broken stapler taped *Do not remove!* A blackboard with a single pink chalk-butt, a dozen graffitied student desks. Light filtered through two plate glass windows, one partly blocked by a shed, the other by maimed rhododendrons edging a muddy lawn.

Oh, what had I done? From the kingdom of infinite pens—Paper Mate, Pilot, Bic; Gel roller, ballpoint, take your pick—to the land of none.

I met the pregnant teacher Dr. Chernov two days before my debut. An Oxford Ph.D. of Elizabethan Literature, she answered none of my questions: Do I lecture, make handouts, discuss? Is there a textbook, reading list, grammar book? And she left me no curriculum, only a book closet key and caveat: "They're stupid, rude and lazy. When they're obnoxious, just deduct points."

I told myself it didn't matter that I'd never headed a classroom. Or written a doctoral thesis on insect imagery in Jacobean poems. Or understood, exactly, who Moshe Ben Maimon was. I wanted to believe my lawyer skills had primed me for teaching. I told myself it would be easy to manage high school students; I was the mother of two teens, and was also the longtime lawyer of the aptly-named magnate Dick Krass. I told myself I'd be inspiring, patient, kind and wise. Still, I fretted like Sister Maria heading down the mountain to the children Von Trapp. *I've always longed for adventure / To do the things I've never dared. / And here I'm facing adventure / Then why am I so scared?*

Because week one, I couldn't pronounce their names: Levi (rhymes with wavy), Dror (where you put your shirts), Uri (rhymes with jury), Channah (as if your throat hurts).

Because week two, I passed out fifty photocopies without even-numbered pages. (Click: letter-sized, *two*-sided, corner-stapled, start.)

Because week three, I misplaced my notes. "So, uh, Rachel, what do you think the little prince means, uh, when he says. . .what was it? 'Straight ahead of him, nobody can go very far. . .'?'"

Because week four, the students dropped their honeymoon façades:

Calling out, as I dictated a spelling quiz, "Hey, Ms. Vallone, have you seen *Shrek* yet?"

Writhing in their seats, as I explained *theme*, "Ms. Vallone, I've got to pee, like *now!*"

Knuckling their nostrils, as I read aloud from *Night*, "Shee-ite, who cut the cheese?"

Because week five, I tried to teach them poetry.

• • • • •

My "Poetry Primer" was a masterpiece—thirteen perfect pages of text, exercises and clip-art sure to spark a passion for Shakespeare. I inserted it into the photocopier (click: letter-sized, *two*-sided, corner-stapled, start). Instantly, warm packets ker-chicked into the tray.

Mark told me I'd worked too hard on it: "Let's eat. It's not a Ninth Circuit brief!" I'd spent nights with *The Norton Anthology* and *The Reader, the Text, the Poem.* I'd spent weekends writing lesson plans. First we'd study imagery, metaphor, alliteration, rhyme. Next we'd read Browning, Rossetti, Dickenson, Shakespeare and Yeats. Then we'd write limericks, sonnets and haikus.

Several days into the unit, the students were scanning the meter of a poem, some crinkling their foreheads, others glancing at the clock, most of them jiggling their legs. I took my place at the lectern. "Okay, time to wrap it up. Yonah, please read the first stanza, stressing the accents so we can hear the beat."

Curly-haired, button-down shirted, he pulsed like a rabbi in prayer. "i WENT out TO the HAzel WOOD / beCAUSE a FIRE was IN my HEAD / and CUT and PEELED a HAZel WAND / and HOOKED a BERry TO a THREAD."

I nodded. "Very good. Leah, please go on."

She frowned, fingered her pink cell phone. "and WHEN white MOTHS were ON the WING / and MOTH-like STARS were FLICKerRING—no, flickERing, FLICKerRING, FLICK!" Eyes blue shards of glass, she slapped her hand on the desk. "I hate poetry! My mother made me study it all summer, and I still don't get it! Your curriculum really sucks!"

Sucks, sucks, sucks. Your curriculum really sucks. A rhythm too complex to scan, a wildfire in my head. *Sucks, sucks, sucks. Your curriculum really sucks.* A mantra scorching me in bed as I stared out the window that night at constellations of Leah's blue-hot eyes.

That night, I wanted to quit teaching, run right back to Turnbull, where some of Seattle's most prominent paid hundreds an hour for my work, listened to what I said. Who do these kids think they are? But while I burned from Leah's glare, conscious of very little else, there was something within it that held me, something in the eyes of all the students that I'd seen in the eyes my own newborns when they first looked up at me. At the time, I couldn't describe it, but now I think I can.

Netzotzim—divine sparks of light. According to Kabbalah, God's light was at first contained in vessels up high in his domain, but it radiated so strongly that the vessels exploded. The fragments fell through the cosmic void, entrapping *netzotzim* within them. They landed far below God's realm, forming our world and its people, a world in which each person contains *netzotzim* within.

The next morning was wind and steely clouds, cat-tracks on frosted grass. I pulled my scarf tighter round my neck as I crossed the school parking lot. Entering the classroom, I flicked on the lights, set my binder down, turned to "Sonnet 13": *O! that you were yourself; But, love, you are / no longer yours—*

The bell rang. I breathed in deeply. The door banged, bodies burst in, books and backpacks thumping on the desks. Galit and Dror approached me, hung their homework like blinds before my eyes.

"Look, I did the questions on 'The Swallow,' and—"

"Ms. Vallone my computer wouldn't print all the pages, so the end is—"

"—'Never Saw a Moor'. Didn't I do good?"

"—handwritten. Is that okay?"

I forced a smile. "Yes, of course! Great work!"

The second bell sent them to their seats, and I picked up my roster pad:

Ephraim, lone desk by computer, opening and closing an ✓
umbrella.

Yonah, behind Ephraim, jamming laptop plug into ✓
outlet.

Dror, left corner, reading *Geeksville*. ✓

Shoshana and Nechemya, front center, sharing ✓✓
earphones, humming.

Galit and Ahava, rear right, gossiping, giggling. ✓✓

Ben, back right corner, desk tipped up precariously off ✓
linoleum.

Tzippy and Aaron, middle center, ogling each other. ✓✓

Leah, nowhere to be found. ✗

I slid my roster under my binder, glanced at my watch. "Okay, everyone, quiet please, umbrellas and desks down, iPods away, books and laptops closed. Please open to 'Sonnet 13'. Who wants to read?"

Palms flew and flailed upward toward florescent lights. Lips moved: "Me, me, me!"

Ben flourished his packet. "O! That you were yourself; but, love—"

Shoshana spun to face him, thick braids whipping round. "Ben, no one called on you!" She swiveled back. "Ms. Vallone, can I read?"

The classroom door squawked open. Leah, a dart in fuchsia Ugg boots, hair riding an air-wave, hurtled into a seat. I eyed her. "Ben, please don't talk unless I call on you. Shoshana, go ahead and read."

"But, love, you are / no longer yours than you yourself here live—"

"Stop it!" I turned, stage left. Tzippy was glaring at Ephraim, his umbrella sliding open and closed. I walked over, pried it from his grip, set it on a shelf.

Shoshana looked their way. "Ahem, can I continue please?" She turned back to her page. "Against this coming end you should prepare, / And your sweet semblance to some other give. . . / then, you were / yourself again, after yourself's decease—"

Thump. I swiveled, stage right. Leah's head was down upon her desk, her arm stretched and dangling off the front. "Oh my God! This so sucks!"

I pressed my lips together. Yes, Leah, I know.

"Freak!" I pivoted, stage left. Ephraim was hunching over Yonah, pointing at the laptop screen. Yonah jabbed him in the ribs. "Get away from me!"

I rolled my eyes. "Ephraim, please sit down! Yonah, close that laptop!" I went to his desk, pulled out the power cord.

"Who lets so fair a house fall to decay, / Which husbandry in honour might uphold / Against the stormy gusts of winter's day / And barren rage of death's eternal cold?"

Giggling, center stage. Tzippy was leaning towards Aaron, felt-tipping hearts upon his page.

"Tzippy, switch seats with Nechemya!"

Doe eyes, quivering lips, she snuggled closer to Aaron. "But I always sit with Aaron. I promise, I'll be quiet."

I pushed back my hair. "Please finish, Shoshana."

"O! none but unthrifts. Dear my love, you know / You had a father: let your son say so."

I nodded. "Good. Now, did any of you see images as Shoshana read? Ben?"

"Yeah, it's a guy who's upset because his girlfriend cheated on him. But she's dying now—maybe she's got cancer—and, uh, the guy's house is falling apart."

Aaron shook his head. "No. It's a mother talking to her son, whose wife is pregnant, and she's telling him to tell his son about his father."

"Whose father?" said Ephraim.

Leah raised her head, pushed herself up to sitting with her arm. "Guys, you're so stupid! It's a husband telling his wife they should have a baby so her beauty won't die out."

And there it was: the turning point. As if God had stopped the action to direct.

Had I heard Leah right? I looked straight into her eyes, a little softer now. "Leah, that's a great interpre—"

Aaron leapt from his seat. "Hey, it's snowing!"

Outside the window, crystal pinwheels spun and tumbled, glittering the grass and rhododendrons. As I watched, desks screeched across the floor, students standing, pushing out the door. They reappeared, laughing and shrieking on the lawn. Raking fingers through the grass, boys gathered snow, shaped and patted balls, then launched them at their friends. Girls twirled like Botticelli's nymphs, long jean skirts swirling round their calves.

Leah, detaching from the dancers, came to the window, tapped. I slid the pane partway open—a glacial gust and faint snow scent.

Her breath made a cloud upon the glass. "Ms. Vallone, that poem was really cool." Then she launched herself from the window, whirling back to her friends. Tilting her chin toward the sky, she reached with her tongue-tip to taste the snowflakes tumbling to the ground.

Perspective

July 2003

I followed the footpath that had been etched into the side of the mountain. Above me hung a canopy of firs, larches and pines, shafts of sunlight flickering through. Cool vapors rose from the earth, scented by pine needles crushed beneath my feet.

Ahead of me trekked my family—Mark unfazed by the sharply-climbing grade, legs methodical, knapsack on his back. Cristin, fifteen, portabrasing with a pink water bottle, her graceful dancer's gait. Sean, thirteen, scouting high and low, severing shoots and roots with his penknife.

I lagged behind the group, losing sight of them when the trail curved, glimpsing them when it straightened, letting the distance grow. When they turned to wait for me, I insistently waved them on. They nodded, vanished into mist.

I leaned on a lightning-scorched tree that had fallen across the path, branches barren, arthritic roots grasping. Redwing thrushes flitted—fir to larch, larch to pine—as if searching for something, calling. Breathing in alpine air, I held it for a moment in my lungs: I'm in the Dolomites. Every cell of my being should be tingling. What is wrong with me?

Days before I'd been humming all morning, my first teaching contract in my pocket, arms lugging shopping bags of hiking gear. I strode up the walkway to our house, reached the old door, fumbled with my keys. Inside, I dropped my parcels, plopped in a living room chair, sunlight through the diamond-light windows making patterns on the floor. It caught the family photos on the mantle, lit the crystal bowl, dazzled the paintings. Still, despite this clutter of things, the room seemed strangely vacant.

I looked around me, then over my shoulder: God, our stereo is gone.

I bolted—up the staircase to the second floor, down the hall to the bedroom. I reached for my dresser drawer, grabbed the knob and pulled. The drawer skated from its hollow, nose-dived to the floor.

The broken lock. The screaming void.

For as long as I could remember, my jewelry had resided in that old oak drawer, carefully locked, the key hidden. Although my family was never wealthy, all the milestones of my life—communion, birthdays, graduations, Christmas, wedding, trips—had been marked with something special, purchased with money scrimped and saved. Whenever I felt lonely, or that I'd accomplished too little in my life, all I had to do was turn the key and slide open the drawer. There, in bits of gold and silver, I'd find reminders of people who'd cared, sometimes of my own worth. Most precious were the family heirlooms—my grandfather's silver pocket-watch, my father's diamond ring, my grandmother's ruby earrings, my mother's strand of pearls. Treasures once part of their bodies, warm, pulsing with life. For me, wearing family jewelry was the embrace of a loved-one long gone.

I bent over the path to tie my bootlace. A finger-sized salamander scurried by, eyes darting to and fro, shiny patent leather skin. He skittered over twigs and gravel, disappeared inside a crevice of a tree. If only I'd hidden my jewelry as well as he hid himself. Why hadn't I listened to my dream? Often it awakened me in the middle of the night, always taking my breath away, making me spring up in bed. Surely, it had been a warning, an insistent ticking bomb.

In the dream, I'm thirteen years old, and it's summer, muggy, hot. I am home alone; my father and mother are working, my friends away at camp, a luxury we can't afford. Longing for some company, I go outside, scope up and down the street. I see no one, but our neighbor Tova's door is open; maybe her beagle Peanuts needs a walk.

I cross the street to Tova's, peer through the metal screen door. She's pacing, talking on the phone, coiled cord stretching and relaxing, binding her to the wall. I rap lightly on the screen. Peanuts leaps out from a corner. He barks and skitters on the floorboards, nails screeching like blackboard chalk. Tova startles, then she sees me, signals *just a minute* with a finger.

I step inside the foyer, pat Peanuts' wriggling body. Through the screen I gaze back at my house—sky cobalt blue. Lawn neon green. Bricks radiating heat. A sudden, fluorescent flash.

A man is fleeing from our house, over the lawn, shooting like an arrow. He hugs a golden coffer to his chest. I scream. He dissolves into the heat.

Once, I'd learned from a news show that prowlers make a beeline for the bedroom, head straight for the woman's dresser drawer. How could I ever have imagined that simply locking mine would be enough? The key was still under my mattress when the thief was cleaning me out.

I proceeded up the footpath, climbed higher through the forest. A waterfall sprang from a cliff, a sudden symphony of sound. Mist cooling my cheeks, I tiptoed over river rocks, crossed a shallow stream. Then I hiked through the shadows of a fir stand, arriving at a meadow, a slope of alpine light.

My family was already seated on a smooth slab jutting from the slope, apples, *pane dei francescani, Asiago* and *Speck* spread before them like a feast. As I approached, Sean licked his fingers, scooted over, making space.

I shook my head at him. "No, Hon, I'm not hungry. I'll sit on that boulder over there," as if ceaseless rumination would bring my jewelry back.

I knew my family was worried I was taking the theft so hard. Before we left on our trip, Mark had daily prodded the police, hoping to recoup my things. Cristin gave me extra hugs and kisses. Sean plied me with diverting conversation. And on the flight to Milan, they badgered me with earphones, made me watch the featured film.

In the movie, American teenager Daphne goes to England to search for her father. She's his by a long-ago lover; he's not aware she exists. In London, she learns her father's famous, a politician from an upper-class family, so she makes her way to his house, scales the garden wall, introduces herself. Smitten by her perkiness, Daphne's British family throws her a debutante ball. On the night of the party, Daphne descends the spiral staircase a-shimmer in a silver gown. When the girl reaches the bottom, her grandmother kisses her forehead and tiaras her hair: "Many years ago, I wore this crown to *my* ball. I'm delighted to pass it down to you."

Daphne hugs her grandma; I volcanoed mucous and tears: "I have nothing left."

As passengers turned to stare at me, Mark gently stroked my hair.

Wandering through meadow grasses, I crossed velvety mosses, crackled lingering crusts of snow. Sitting on the surface of the boulder, I hugged my knees to my chest. Warmth penetrated my body from smooth stone and limpid sun, wild thyme scent ascending. Poppies, gentians, lilies winked at me—yellow, blue, orange in a visage of green. I looked across the meadow at the pines through which I'd trekked. They were silver as my grandfather's pocket-watch. The kind called a *savonette*, hinged cover protecting its crystal, fob link at three o'clock, I'd loved to wind that watch, watch its hands circle its face, listen to its tick, tick, tick.

The summer I was eight, my grandfather took us grandkids to the Freeport fishing pier—my cousins Angela and Nick, my little sister Pat and me. Each of us carried a pail, salt water sloshing out the top, and we laughed as it splattered our legs, wet our shorts and sprinkled the boards. Ahead of us walked Grampa, toting a tackle box and fishing rods, head shining in the sunlight like a Benedictine's tonsure. When we reached the end of the pier, he pulled his pocket watch—glint— from his shorts. Grampa smiled and nodded, "Plenty of time to fish."

My grandfather loved to fish and it was no wonder; he'd grown up in Castellammare on Sicily's western coast. There, as a boy, he'd fished with nets from a wooden dingy. But in Freeport he never used nets. Rather, he opened up his tackle box, strung hooks and sinkers on our rods, baited them with mackerel, his stubby tailor fingers nimble. One by one, he released our reel locks, lasso-flicked our rods, lines arcing over our heads and unspooling into the sea.

He handed each of us a rod. "If you want to catch a fish, you need to be quiet. Don't move, and when you feel a tug, do this." He cranked a reel to whirring, winding hook and sinker from the water. "Can you do that?"

We nodded, then waited. Waited, silent, still. I shifted my weight from foot to foot, seagulls swooping and crying, sun burning my cheeks, sweat stinging my eyes.

Tug. My rod suddenly flexing, tip almost touching the sea. I tottered, pulled back, regaining my balance. "Grampa, I think I caught a fish!"

He motioned with his rod. "Quick, Kid, reel 'er in!"

Weight bobbing on the line, rod bending like a bow, I cranked the reel round and round. The fish flipped from the sea like a puppet dancing on a string. I jerked it onto the pier.

It gasped and thrashed on the boards, bulging eyes plucking my heart. Grampa picked it up, wrenched the hook from its kissing mouth. "Look kids, she's a blowfish." He laid her gently on his palm, tickled her tummy; it swelled to a sequined balloon. Grampa looked at us and smiled. "Amazing, isn't she? But she's poisonous—we can't eat 'er—so we have to throw 'er back."

Grampa cast the blowfish from the pier. She flashed silver, slipped into the sea, wriggled, righted, swam free.

I sat up straighter on the boulder, pressed my forehead to my knees. What right did that creep have to break our basement window, wander through our house, open my drawer and rummage through my things? A few days after the burglary, his ex-girlfriend reported him, and a policeman drove her to our house to confirm the scene of the crime. That's when we learned the burglar's name: Martin Jinks, a gunrunner, drug dealer, addict, a felon with wild red hair. He'd boasted to his girlfriend about the heist at our home—"Lawyers! I saw their diplomas!" Then, promptly, he skipped town.

Martin, how I hate you. What have I done to deserve this? How could you take my grandfather's watch? Where did you pawn my grandmother's earrings?

I loved my grandmother's earrings—ruby teardrops from the twenties set in gold, so prized I rarely wore them, but my grandmother rarely took them off.

Hen-bodied, four-foot-ten, Gramma was fabled for her cooking. For my tenth birthday she made a special meal: sliced tomato *antipasto*, lasagna with extra mozzarella (to Gramma, "moohtsadell"), *spiedini di vitello, cannoli* stuck with candles. Peeking out from her kitchen, she smoothed her apron with her hands. "Time to eat!" Then she pointed to our places at her table, eyeing Angela, Nick, Pat and me: "Soon you kids will be so tall, you'll eat spaghettis off my head!"

As always, when everyone was seated, she served my grandfather first, watching him take his first bite, pressing her lips together thin. He chewed theatrically, slowly, jaw revolving round and around. And just when his Adam's apple bulged, Gramma blurted her signature remark: "It's good, isn't it!"

Grampa mulled over her words as if he hadn't heard them each day for forty years. "It's good, Es...but please—please, don't make it again!"

"*Salute!*" Everybody clinked wine or Coca Cola glasses, Gramma shaking her head, ruby earrings twinkling like the stained glass at Saint Christopher's Church.

Earlier that day, she asked me to help with the tomatoes. Banging cupboards and drawers, she grabbed knife, cutting board, platter, placed them on the counter, found olive oil, basil, salt, pepper, set them by the sink. Colander in hand, she marched out the back door.

Screen door clapping behind me, I followed her into the yard— patio baking in the sun, iron table, scattered lawn chairs. Mimosa reaching for the sky, feathered fronds, fragrant pink puffs. Tomato vines climbing the fence laced on sisal twine. Gramma kneeled before the vines. "If you want to make a good salad, choose red tomatoes, no green." She lifted a bract of leaves, exposing a ruby tomato, snapped it from the stem and handed it to me.

Alpine breeze ruffling the meadow, a ladybug lighted on my shoulder; I sat still watching her preen. Dainty head, threadlike legs, she fluffed black-spotted red wings. Once Angela had told me I should never brush a ladybug away; each was the Virgin Mary come to bring good luck. Lady, is it true? Will you bring back my jewelry? At least my father's wedding ring? I'd loved to slip it on my finger, flutter a diamond-light dance.

When I was twelve years old, my father planned a trip to Italy, one he'd fantasized for years. My mother, Pat and I had never been on an airplane; my father, not since World War Two. But often, on the weekends, he'd take us to Kennedy Airport (which he, a staunch Republican, never stopped calling Idlewild). There, we'd watch take-offs and landings like other families watched T.V. :

He, pointing at the runway: "Look, a DC-8! Four engines. Isn't she a beauty?"

We, nodding in unison: "Uh, huh. Very nice."

On our departure day, he again drove us to the airport, this time singing with Dean Martin:

"*Volare*, oh oh;

Cantare, oh oh oh oh.

Let's fly way up to the clouds,

Away from the maddening crowds."

Tapping steering wheel with ring, he scattered diamond rainbows round the car—ceiling, dashboard, backseat—Pat and I trying to catch them—red, orange, gold, green, blue and mauve.

He parked at the T.W.A. Building, a concrete dove in flight, checked our baggage, led us onto the plane. We followed a stewardess to our seats. Then my father turned to my mother. "I'll sit behind with Jan. You sit here with Pat."

He pointed me into the window seat, slid into its mate, leaned over me to look out the window. "Nice. Right over the wings."

The plane taxied over the tarmac. I pulled my seatbelt tight. We merged in a long queue of rudder art—a gold sun on blue for Lufthansa, red, white and green for Alitalia, a cobalt globe for Pan Am. One by one, planes nosed into the air.

Our plane lurched onto the runway, gathered speed. It lifted nose, then tail. Closing my eyes, I clutched the armrests: Dear God, please keep us safe.

Dad patted my hand, a brief, awkward staccato. "Kiddo, open your eyes. See the air-streams rushing round the wings? They're so cold they look like frost. They create a special force that keeps the airplane safe.

It's called Bernoulli's principle."

I looked out the window. The streams embraced us like an angel, the sky, bright and clear, the Atlantic scattering light.

When the police fingerprinted our house, they said I'd likely not retrieve my jewelry. Thieves normally pluck out the gems, melt down the metals, then sell the lot. What's the point of having treasures if someone can trash them just like that? My father's wedding ring, molten. My mother's pearls, severed beads. I'd worn them almost daily, sacred as a rosary to me. Why hadn't I worn them that day? How had Martin known I'd left them home?

When I was two years old, my parents bought a lot on Long Island. While our house was under construction, we'd go there weekends to inspect—"Beeyooteeful Baldwin!" the train conductor always said. The foundation was dug into the sand, a short walk from the beach. In a photo, we sit among the pilings—Mom, sun-dressed on a blanket, pearls bright around her neck. Pat cradled on her lap, moonfaced, fast asleep. Dad in baggy paisley swim trunks, me in a skirted bathing suit. Sandwiches and curvy-bottled Cokes spread on a cloth in the sand.

After we moved into our house, Mom liked to walk upon the beach, short black curls blowing on the breeze, lipsticked smile, slightly buck teeth. When I was six, she took me clamming. We padded barefoot at the sea-edge, Mom singing my favorite song:

"Smile and the world smiles with you;

Cry and you cry alone.

My dear, little Jan,

Always smile and be happy!"

Skirting seaweed, dead crabs and driftwood, we left a trail of footprints snaking far behind us, sand coating my legs, my shorts gritty, wet. Every once in a while, a wave rolled out and lapped me clean.

Mom, carrying a pail, bent her head, scanned the tidal mud flats. "Clams live in the muck. They squirt water out of their bodies like they're blowing through a straw. We can find them by looking for their holes. Look, see them here?"

Mom set down her pail, pressed her toes into the muck. She cupped her feet like trowels, then began to dig: left, right, left. Grit flew from side to side, water filling the hollows as she dug. When she'd gone down several inches, she reached into the puddle she'd made. "Here."

She placed a clam on my palm. It pulled in its worm-like siphon like a miser taking money from a bank and clamped its pearly shell shut like a woman snapping closed her purse.

From my boulder, I looked beyond the meadow at a velvet valley buttoned with chalets, church steeple pricking up. The village was so far below me, it seemed like Lilliput. A ring of glacial peaks surrounded it and me, pressing into the sky, tops lost in the clouds. I tilted back my head, gazed up: Oh, how tiny I am. A fragment of Creation, a flicker in all-time. Even more miniscule are my trinkets, wherever on Earth they are. If I could spread them out before me, they would not outshine these mountains, this sky. What do I need them for?

Up the slope, the clanging of cowbells. Bounding down, a ram, a ewe, two lambs. As I watched, my family scrambled from their roost, laughing, meeting the sheep.

Sean stroked the ram's back, turned to me: "Mom, c'mon. They're cool!"

Mark rummaged in his backpack, pulled out his camera and lens.

Cristin dodged the nuzzling lambs. "Yuck! Make them go away!"

I stood, brushed the seat of my shorts, crossed the meadow to my family.

Part II

A man who was going on a journey called in his servants
and entrusted his possessions to them.
To one he gave five talents. . . Then he went away.
Immediately the one who received five talents went and
traded with them, and made another five.
After a long time the master of those servants came back
and settled accounts with them.
The one who had received five talents came forward
bringing the additional five. He said, "Master, you
gave me five talents. See, I have made five more."
His master said to him, "Well done, my good and faithful
servant. Since you were faithful in small matters, I
will give you great responsibilities. Come, share your
master's joy."

—Matthew 25: 14-16, 19-21

• • • • •

There are four types among those who sit before the sages:
the sponge, the funnel, the strainer and the sieve.
The sponge absorbs all.
The funnel takes in at one end and lets it out the other.
The strainer rejects the wine and retains the sediment.
The sieve rejects the coarse flour and retains the fine flour.

—Pirkei Avot: 5.15

A Greater Peace

January 2005

I entered the tiny classroom, and the door closed softly behind me. Sunlight streamed through the windows; fresh paint glowed. I surveyed the familiar surroundings. The Rabbi's books—Torah, Siddur Ha-Shalem—were still jumbled on the top tiers of the bookshelf; mine—*Night, Romeo and Juliet*—stood towards the bottom in rows. At the front of the room, a battered oak lectern beckoned. I approached it, set a thick candle on top, turned to watch the second hand pulse around the clock.

The bell rang. A cacophony of voices in the schoolyard. Girls squealed: "Hey, Shoshana!" "Whoa, Rachel!" Boys shouted: "Slap five, Yonah!" "My man, Ben!" I smoothed the long skirt I'd purchased to meet the dress code, emotions spiraling, ascending—delight, determination, dread.

Kappah—the door burst open. Hwoosh—in swept the class. First a whirling dervish girl, jeweled Star of David swinging from her neck. Next a boy with an athlete's gait and *yarmulked* red hair. Then a swirling tangle of bodies giving rise to a chaos of color and noise. They kissed the doorframe *mezuzah*, banged backpacks on desks, flung lithe bodies into sculpted plastic seats, eying me up and down.

The second bell rang, then silence. I scanned the room from face to face. Oh, so very young—the shy, the genial, the cocky. The jokers, demons, saints. Oh, the Cristins, the Seans—all waiting to be known. As was I.

I smiled. "Hi everyone. Welcome to high school. In a moment, I'll ask you to introduce yourselves, but first, I'm Ms. Vallone and this"—I pointed like Houdini—"is my candle." I briskly struck a match and lit it, the faint scent of peaches wafting in the air. "As you can see, it creates a tiny bit of light. Can anyone tell me how much light there'd be if I gave each of you a candle and lit them all with mine?"

Boys in the back row smirked: What a stupid question! But a girl with long dark corkscrew hair cocked her head thoughtfully, said, "A lot more light?"

I nodded. "A lot more light. And how much light would there be if each of you went out into the world, gave everyone you met a candle and lit each one with yours?"

Hands darted up, emboldened. Voices called, "Even more light!"

"Good, even more light. Now, what do you think my candlelight symbolizes? After all, this is Language Arts, and we'll be dealing with symbols all year."

Some students exchanged glances. Other knit eyebrows together. I tapped my temple with my finger, watched the cogs as they turned.

A brown-eyed boy with dark lashes inched a pinkie towards the ceiling. "Knowledge?"

"Yes. And one more thing?" Raising my hand to my shoulder, I formed a V with my middle and index fingers.

A girl, Tinkerbell tiny, bobbed up from a desk at the front. "Oh, I know! Peace?"

I smiled. "Yes, peace. My candlelight symbolizes knowledge and peace, because candlelight, knowledge and peace all work the same. If I use my flame to light others, I create a greater light. If I use my knowledge to teach others, I create a deeper understanding. If I treat others with respect, I create a broader tolerance. And if each of you and those you meet does the same, we create a world of light, knowledge, peace."

Some students rolled their eyes—God, this teacher's corny! Others students smiled—Oh, this teacher's sweet!

I looked into their faces. "That's why I'm here—to teach you Language Arts, the art of communication. And I hope you'll use your learning to make a difference in the world, promote a greater peace. I hope you'll take my tiny flame, add it to yours, use it to light the flames of others."

"No offense, Ms. Vallone," said a boy in a Yankees jacket sitting in the rear, "but what if you don't believe in peace? What if you think some people aren't worth talking to—people who are better off dead?"

Boy chuckles, glint of braces. Girl eyes shooting darts at boys. But I knew he was serious, his comment common at the school. Bristling, I blew out the candle, pretended not to hear.

But I didn't feel right about it. How many violent pictures had been etched into my memory during my school days? White firemen hosing black picketers in Birmingham, Alabama. A rider-less horse at the White House, boots backwards in its stirrups. Naked, napalmed children fleeing a Vietnam village. A Kent State coed kneeling and shrieking over a classmate's corpse. And how many more images had been added since my students started school? Amber flames bursting from planes exploding the Twin Towers. A row of massive crosses casting shadows at Columbine High. I'd been waiting for the peace train since the sixties, yet let it pass me with the comment of that boy.

If I worked at a public high school, I'd have confronted the student directly, chided him for his comment. I'd have told him in my classroom, we'd practice inclusion—tolerance in word and deed. Which is not only what I believe in, but what public schools strive to teach—at least theoretically. But I'd learned that at Moshe Ben Maimon, *exclusion* was the goal in many ways, assimilation denounced (one poster in the office pictured a bug labeled *assimilation*, a shoe about to step on it). Only Jewish students were admitted, *Jewish* strictly defined: children born to Jewish mothers, Jewish by matrilineal descent. If Mom wasn't Jewish, you were out, even if Dad was Jewish, even if you practiced Judaism. Then, once you were in the school, you studied Judaism daily, eight to noon, under the tutelage of darkly-dressed rabbis and their head-bescarfed wives, who grounded your learning in the Torah:

When the Lord, your God, brings you into the land [of Israel], which you are to enter and occupy, and dislodges great nations before you—

And when the Lord, your God, delivers them up to you and you defeat them, you shall doom them. Make no covenant with them and show them no mercy.

Which gave rise to certain corollaries: You must conquer, defend, and develop the land of Israel, not allow Gentiles to possess it. You must not travel or be alone with a Gentile. You must not date or become too close to a Gentile. You must not seek medical treatment from a Gentile. You must not eat foods prepared by a Gentile. You must focus exclusively on the welfare of Jews, not dissipate time or funds on Gentiles.

So, at Moshe Ben Maimon, teaching inclusion went only so far, lest you wound up displaying intolerance of your students' exclusionist beliefs. Ashamed as I am to admit it, there were times I kept my mouth shut—when bodily harm or personal insult wasn't a threat—times I settled for bristling for fear of supporting the wrong people (Arabs? Blacks? Christians? Gays?), for fear of losing my job. To be as true to my beliefs as I could, I opted for the subtle: lighting my candle each fall, stressing communication, helping my students peek over the fence by assigning non-Jewish literature in addition to Jewish fare. And I rationalized—with guilt for both my arrogance and meekness—that what I did for tolerance was more than my students would otherwise get.

But it wasn't always easy, as on one Friday several weeks into the school year. The freshmen had been studying memoir and were writing stories of their own. I looked up at the clock, realized class was about to end. "Okay, everyone. Time to wrap it up. And before you leave, please remember to turn in your drafts. I—"

The bell rang. A chorus of zippers and chatter as the students leapt like hares before a shotgun. They tossed their work in my basket, grabbed their backpacks, dashed. They raced to make it home before Shabbat, which starts each Friday at sundown, when working, riding in cars, turning on electricity and using phones are banned till the first three stars of Saturday appear in the evening sky.

Judith lingered, dancer-dainty, hugging her books to her chest. She approached as I gathered the memoirs.

I peeked up. "Judith, can I help you with something?"

She looked down at her books. "Ms. Vallone…are you Jewish?"

How I dreaded this question. Someone asked it every year. "No, I'm not."

She ground her sneaker toe into the floor. "Then…what are you?"

I breathed in for confession. "I'm Catholic, Judith."

She gazed out the window. "Oh…That's too bad. Well, *Shalom Shabbat* anyway." And she smiled, scurried out the door.

I remember one fall day when I was Judith's age. It was a crisp morning, the sky crystal blue. I sat on the front steps of our split-level house on Long Island that looked like all the others, idling on Yom Kippur, a day off from our school. As I watched, all of our neighbors passed under sugar maples, penumbras of burning bush color, making their pilgrimage to Temple Shaarei Shalom. My mother always said she knew they were God's chosen people—on *their* holidays it was always sunny. On *ours,* it always rained.

I had been to the synagogue on very few occasions, for the bar mitzvahs of our neighbors' sons, solemn ceremonies in incomprehensible Hebrew—*Barukh atah Adonai, Eloheinu, melekh ha-ola*—followed by lavish receptions fragrant with *latkes,* beef brisket, white roses. There, I'd dizzily danced the hora in a whirling circle holding hands, first tugging right, then tripping left, then pulling arms up towards the center shouting Woo!, reveling in the rare miracle of being one of the group.

One mid-December evening when I was fifteen, though, I learned I'd never feel that way again—at least not in Baldwin. Pacing the kitchen floor, I was on the phone with my friend Rina when my mother came home. She placed groceries bags on the counter, turned on the radio softly, Barbra Streisand suffusing Rina's news.

Barbra: "Have yourself a merry little Christmas; let your heart be light. From now on, our troubles will be out of sight. . ."

Rina: "My mother called the temple about the Chanukah dance and asked if I could bring you."

Me: "What did they say?"

Barbra: "Faithful friends who are dear to us gather near to us once more. Through the years, we all will be together, if the Fates allow. . ."

Rina: "I'm really sorry, but you have to be Jewish to go."

Me: "But everyone will be there!"

Barbra: "Hang a shining star upon the highest bough, and have yourself a merry little Christmas now."

Rina: "I tried. Really!"

My mother, having eavesdropped, was folding the shopping bags when I hung up. She slammed them on the table: "The nerve! Meanwhile, a Jew is making millions singing Christmas songs!"

I ran from the room, crying, "God, I hate it here!"

Even so, perched on my stoop, I waved to the Lieber family as they passed, called, "*G'mar chatimah tovah.*"—"May you be sealed for a good year in the Book of Life." They nodded, turned around the corner, disappeared. With the toe of my shoe, I flicked a small displaced stone to join the others in the garden bed. Then I stood, turned my back and went inside, wondering if I'd ever find a place where I belonged.

• • • • •

Had my parents been alive, they'd have been shocked I worked at a yeshiva. Though they'd had many Jewish friends, they sometimes made comments in private I didn't understand when I was young, later regarded as hypocritical and still later guessed grew out of jealousy. Our Jewish neighbors drove the Cadillacs in Baldwin, wore the diamonds and gold, and in December menorahs outshined Christmas trees fifty to one. Then came the matter of friendship when my sister and I reached high school. There were so few Gentiles in our public school that we were left alone when our Jewish girlfriends paired with Jewish boys, to all of whom we were taboo. So I think each of us in my family secretly wished to be something we weren't: either chosen or chosen by the chosen. Maybe it's ironic, but I loved my yeshiva students—Akiva, Miri, Shoshana, Tmima, Elisheva, Zach. Maybe part of me hoped they'd heal my past by loving me back, as maybe my father had hoped Carol Cohen would heal his.

So that Friday afternoon as the freshmen went off for Shabbat, I set out for Starbucks to grade their work. Sitting near the hearth with a coffee, I began to read their memoirs. First I picked up Chelsea's writing:

> I started talking with Matthew and Christine. Our conversation was only a few simple words with little meaning. Just sounds to pass the time. "Oh my gosh, guys, Mrs. Swift gave me so much homework!" I complained.
> "God, Chelsea, you're such a stupid Jew."
> I felt like I had been pushed to the ground. I gasped heavily for air that wouldn't come. I forgot what we were talking about, and my only thought was: Did Matthew really say that?

Next Jack's:

> I banged my head against the wall on purpose. Why did I confuse myself so much? Maybe it would help me understand?

I'd thought about it until my brain was weak. Where was the little boy that I'd once been—joyful, friendly, secure? Replaced by a person that I barely knew—angry, anti-social, unsure—filled up with hate, lies and emptiness. I wanted to be whole again, home again—but I didn't know where home was. . .

Then Mira's:

Normally I don't find sleeping on an airplane to be a problem. This flight was different. In a few hours, I would land in Israel. Israel—the place where everyone was Jewish and all the food was kosher—the place where everyone had a special connection with each other and with history. Israel was the land of my people that I had been taught about for as long as I could remember, but had never once seen outside of dreams . . .

Dropping the stories on my lap, I rubbed my temples, closed my eyes. *Pushed to the ground, whole again, Israel, land of my dreams. Such a stupid Jew, my people, I'm confused, please take me home.* Could it be my students felt as foreign in the broad world—mine—as I felt in theirs? After all, they lived cloistered in one neighborhood so they could walk to synagogue on Shabbat, while *kashrut* barred them from eating in most restaurants in town. And many were the grandchildren of Holocaust survivors, aware of their people's historic persecution.

Having grown up in a Jewish neighborhood meant I'd lived in the Holocaust's shadow, my neighbors often whispering their grief. I'd read Anne Frank's diary in grade school, knew about the Nazis, about the death camps, the six million Jews. My neighbors boycotted German products—nary a Beetle on the streets. And they complained when Mrs. Perlemann began the *Deutsch* class at our school.

Then there was The Box, a battered mahogany humidor on the Goldbergs' coffee table. Whenever I went to play with Larry, he'd slide it towards me to make space for our Monopoly board. He'd look somberly at me. "Don't touch The Box. It's from the Holocaust."

I probably wouldn't have cared about The Box had Larry said nothing about it, but its *verboten*ess made it magnetically repellant. Still, I dared not touch or ask. But one Monopoly day when we were eleven, Larry got out of jail after a long incarceration. As he headed toward Saint James Place, he bumped the board with his hand. The Box fell on the rug, lid tumbled, contents spilling out.

We gaped at them for a moment, rubberneckers viewing roadside carnage—black and white snapshots with saw-tooth edges, scattered on the floor. Then Larry began to collect them. "My relatives took these in the Holocaust. They were prisoners at Buchenwald. It's in Germany. The photos were smuggled out so people would know what was going on."

One by one, he held them out to me. Hollow-eyed men peering through a barbed-wire fence. Prisoners in striped pajamas lugging railroad ties. Cadavers piled on a platform, foot bottoms towards the camera. A dead boy Larry's and my age stretched out in the mud.

My stomach wrenched. My throat constricted. I wanted to throw up.

Larry slipped the pictures in their coffin. Then he closed the lid.

I couldn't sleep after The Box. The images blistered my mind, but like most things faded with time—until the next summer, my family's first trip abroad. Sun an orange disk in sky, we were cooling at a Rome motel pool when another family arrived. They nodded, dropped their towels on lounge chairs. The son—blond, about my age—stood at the pool's edge, tugged his black Speedo. Then stretching arms overhead, he smiled, "*Guten Tag!*," leapt, flashing blue laser eyes at me. Instantly afraid as he splashed into the water, I clambered out of the pool, pulled my towel round me, rushed back to our room.

No wonder my students seemed wary, sometimes hostile to non-Jewish people. No wonder they doubted peace.

On Monday I stood before the class. "Hi everyone, I have to tell you—you did a great job on your memoirs. But writing them is just the first step. Now you have to revise them, make them perfect. I'll give you all the help you need. Then, in January, instead of having a final, we're all going to Starbucks. We'll invite friends and family and host a fireside reading. I've already arranged it with the manager and cleared it with Rabbi Schwartz."

Nava raised her eyebrows. "You mean we have to read in public?"

I nodded. "Uh, huh,"

"No way! My story's awful!"

A chorus: "So's mine!"

"Mine too."

Omer shook his head, folding his arms on his chest. "I've got nothing to say. I'm not reading."

Chelsea put her paper in a folder. "We're, sorry, Ms. Vallone, but we don't want to read."

I stared at my students, and they looked back at me. How I wanted them to find their voices, their places in the world. "Listen, everyone— your memoirs are amazing. When I read them, I was moved. You need to realize something. We all live in the same world and have the same emotions—love, grief, loneliness. People have been telling stories about them ever since Adam and Eve. Those stories help us understand each other, and yours do the same. When I read them, I saw myself. Other people will too."

Silence. Nobody moved.

"Remember my candle? Well, maybe you think it's silly, but I'm serious about it. Please go home and do your revisions."

On a cold winter morning, sky of flannel gray, I stood at the front door of a Starbucks that looked like all the rest. I watched as my students climbed down from a bus and filed inside the coffee house. Within, a circle of plush armchairs had been arranged around the hearth. Sitting and standing about was a crowd of chatting people—

teens, adults, children—hot chocolates and coffees in hand. When they saw the students, they made room and quieted down.

Nava came forward, ponytail swinging, eyes cast down. "Welcome—welcome to our reading."

Someone whistled; the crowd began to clap.

Nava looked up cautiously, eyelashes fluttering her bangs. "We hope you like our reading. Please relax and enjoy."

One by one, the students came forward. Mira, Jack, Chelsea. Isaac, Shira, Omer. Sarah, Avraham, Rachel. They read their stories to their parents. They read to friends, to strangers, and to me. And as they did, the crowd around them nodded, exchanging glances, clapping in between.

I waved to my students later as they departed in their bus. Jack pushed down a window, thrust out his hand, formed a V with his fingers: "That was amazing, Ms. Vallone," his words vaporizing into frigid air.

Communion

December 2004

Dark clouds churned low over the freeway, dropping torrents of rain. Cars and trucks sped by on either side of my car—Peterbilt flatbeds hauling fifty-foot logs, mom-driven Hummers ferrying children to school, B.M.W.s piloted by men with Bluetooth headsets—all spraying mud from their tires. My wipers pulsed steadily but uselessly, a gritty pendulum smearing my windshield and obscuring the road.

How I hated December.

The weather was only part of it. That morning I'd made myself a list: Grade poems, read Gardner, write lesson plan. Sean's tournament, Cristin's project, fridge repair. Mark's party, dry clean dress, call vet. And on top of it all was Christmas. Shopping, cards, decorations. Baking, cooking, guests. Not that I really did that much anymore. Each year I dropped something else. Gone were lights on the house. Banished, the banister greens. The crèche remained in storage. I wished we could skip the tree. Why waste a month pretending something special was going to happen? What, Christmas Eve Mass? Standing for two hours in an over-crowded church, listening to children sing off-key? Wishing peace to strangers right on cue, praying to a wooden Holy Family?

Thank goodness Mark enjoyed shopping. Ever the faithful provider, he'd taken it over years before—soliciting lists from our children, his mother and sister, her family. Sneaking downtown to Nordstrom, Barnes and Noble, Old Navy, the Bon Marché. Wrapping presents in fancy foiled papers, tying bows, curling ribbons, tagging boxes. Hiding the gifts in his closet, nestled behind his gym bags. Slipping them out on Christmas Eve after our kids fell asleep.

Mark, the perfect Father Christmas.

And oh, how our children loved it. "Thank you, Dad!" they squealed each Christmas morning, ogling the loot beneath the tree, ripping through reams of paper, tossing it like confetti. At this, Mark's eyes would gleam. Every year, it encouraged me.

"Cristin, Sean," I'd say. "You've opened plenty of presents. How about our gift for Dad?"

Flanneled butts bobbing under boughs, they'd search for the box with his nametag: Not this one. Not that one. Not this. Faces emerging and smiling, they'd hold out the gift to Mark, "Here, Dad, for you!"

Mark would glance at me quickly, set the gift on his lap. Then he'd un-stick each strip of tape, never tearing the paper, and I'd search his face for a sign. Maybe this year he'll like it and say, "Wow, everybody! Thanks!"

But most years when the paper fell away, Mark's eyes would darken, his features rocky as Mount Rushmore. He'd look up. "Uh, huh. Very nice."

And then I'd look away. Another bomb of a gift.

For the rest of Christmas Day, he'd retreat to the playroom with the kids and the toys he'd given, and I'd exile myself to the kitchen with the turkey where I belonged. Throughout the afternoon, I'd check the location of the gift. If it moved from the tree before dinner, it meant I'd misunderstood; Mark had decided to keep it, sequestered it safe among his things. But if it stayed among the piles of paper, as it did most every year, it meant he'd decided to return it. Then we'd play our game: Next day, he'd sneak the gift out of the house when he thought I wasn't looking, and I'd feign ignorance.

On twenty-three consecutive Christmases, I swore I'd never buy Mark a gift again. But always at the last moment, hope would rise like Scylla from the sea, a monster I just couldn't vanquish, and I'd race from store to store, drunk with Christmas Musak—*on the first day of Christmas, my true love gave to me*—determined to get it right, find a gift fit for a king. Maybe a Patagonia shirt or silk Italian tie. Maybe a Miles Davis C.D. or a bike odometer. But, every Christmas morning, hope would smash upon the rocks. Christmas was a senseless obligation—*and a partridge in a pear tree.*

As I exited off the freeway, the rain was letting up some, clouds were rising, but the wind was wild. Fir and cedar branches skittered on the street, leaving wet needle streaks behind. I checked my dashboard clock. I'd make it just in time to get to Moshe Ben Maimon before my students.

My students. Now there was an interesting bunch. Their lives were filled with obligations, duties the staff of life. The first thing they did at school each morning was report to the *Beit Midrash,* a synagogue lined with books—Torah, Siddurim, Shulchan Aruch. Talmud, Mishneh Torah, Arbaah Turim. There, before the Star of David, they gathered for *shacharit,* boys in *yarmulkes* and prayer shawls, standing between the main-floor pews, swaying their bodies back and forth. Girls huddled in the mezzanine smoothing their ankle-length skirts, everybody chanting:

"V'ahav'ta eit Adonai	"And you shall love the Lord
Elohekha b'khol l'vav'kha	your God with all your heart
uv'khol naf'sh'kha uv'khol	and with all your soul and
m'odekha.	with all your might.
V'hayu had'varim ha'eileh	And these words that I
asher anokhi m'tzav'kha	command you today shall be
hayom al l'vavekha.	in your heart.
V'shinan'tam l'vanekha	And you shall teach them
v'dibar'ta bam b'shiv't'kha	diligently to your children,
b'veitekha uv'lekh't'kha	and you shall speak of them
vaderekh uv'shakh'b'kha	when you sit at home, and
uv'kumekha."	when you walk along the
	way, and when you lie down
	and when you rise up…"

The *Shema.* My students lived that prayer. God was their life, those shalls their purpose. Each day after *shacharit,* they spent four hours studying Judaics—Talmud, Torah SheBe'Al Peh, Chumash,

Halacha, Navi—striving to learn the laws God gave Moses at Mount Horeb, all six hundred thirteen. Then, starting at noon, they began the secular curriculum: science, history, foreign language, math and language arts. Nine classes per day, they raced from one to the next, three minutes between periods, no snack or bathroom break. And each time they entered a classroom, they tapped and kissed the *mezuzah*, a small encased prayer scroll inscribed with the *Shema* affixed to every doorframe in the school. Tap-kiss. Tap-kiss. Tap-kiss. All day long until *mincha*, afternoon prayers.

And their holidays never ended, five in autumn alone. On Rosh Hashanah a ram's horn called them to empty their pockets in a river, symbolically casting off their sins. On Yom Kippur they fasted for atonement, smelling spices to endure. During Sukkot they ate and slept in makeshift huts loosely thatched with reeds and gazed up at the stars like the ancient Israelites in the desert. On Simchat Torah they finished the annual cycle of reading through the Torah, dancing to rejoice. During Chanukah they lit candles to mark the miraculous recapture of Solomon's Temple from the Greeks.

In truth, I envied my students. How wonderful to believe in God so deeply that rituals seem meaningful, worth the time. How comforting to feel that someone—God, community—values endeavors, gives purpose to life. How marvelous to be connected with a history, a people, the divine. How sweet to believe in miracles.

When I was young, I too believed in God. I prayed every night on my knees, went to Mass each Sunday, observed the Roman Catholic rites. I remember my First Communion—walking in line with first-grade girls entering from the left, boys flowing from right. Stepping in time to the organ—right-left-pause, left-right-pause, right-left-pause. Veiled girls in frothy white dresses, crew-cut boys in tidy blue suits, all dangling rosaries from dimpled prayer-clasped hands. I felt somehow bound to my classmates as our lines merged at the center aisle and we filed forward, like Noah's creatures toward the ark. And when I took my seat, I focused on the altar, kept my body still, as Sister Clara had showed us. I believed submission would please God and make my parents proud, trusted I was part of God's plan, that my actions mattered in Heaven and made a difference here on Earth. And oh, the host upon my tongue, a melting miracle in my mouth, my heart expanding, mind wheeling, body floating through, with and in God.

All throughout my youth, I could summon that feeling just by closing my eyes, breathing fresh air, lighting a candle, humming a hymn. I felt it one summer evening as I walked the beach at thirteen. Day beginning to fade, sky streaked pink and tangerine, seagulls circled overhead, their wingtips black, their breasts white. They swooped whimsical zigzags, sometimes kissing the sea, then rose to rejoin the flock. Calling, they seemed to know their purpose. Longing to know mine too, that night I asked God in a poem:

> starlight, moonlight top waves with hats of silver
> shining, gleaming out to eternity
> beauteous visions begin to hypnotize our minds
> with wondering questions
> why should all this be?
> birds are laughing, roaming free above us
> happy, thankful to own the sky and sea
> sharing with us the marvels of the wondrous world
> living, loving, the joy of being free.
> answers, reasons begin to flow within us
> reaching, grasping, wanting so to see
> show us, tell us, God, please let us know why
> You gave us Creation, unworthy as we be.

In those days, I never doubted God's existence; the world's beauty was his testament. But I knew it wasn't free: Sister Agnes had told us to be worthy, we had to live the words Jesus once taught to a lawyer named Luke:

You shall love the Lord, your God, with all your heart, with all your being, with all your strength, and with all your mind, and your neighbor as yourself. Do this and you will live.

Loving God, she explained, meant serving other people with our talents, always putting others first. Living meant being loved and also bearing the cross.

Work, serve, and you shall be loved. I believed this when I left for college. There, I vowed to work hard to serve God and please my parents. I'd discover my talents and hone them, use them to earn my share of love. Then one day, I'd stand before a crowd, dressed in dazzling white. A man would hang a medal round my neck, my name inscribed in its gold. Or maybe he'd give me a trophy, perhaps an etched crystal bowl. The crowd would cheer and applaud, and my father would rush to my side. He'd wrap his arm around my shoulders, speak into the microphone: "This is my wonderful daughter. I'm so pleased with her."

I spent my college years studying, declining party invitations. But whenever I earned an A, I took my bicycle out of storage and cruised the Chenango Valley with my study-partner Gerry. He always rode at the fore, enjoying the primacy of leading. I always kept him in sight while remaining far behind. In the fall we coursed the wooded hills, he, on his orange ten-speed, me, on my yellow three, straining to reach the crests, where the view would open up—red-gold maples, green balsam firs. There I'd slow to tottering on top, smile at the sky, sun warming my cheeks, then plunge down the descent, zigzagging under boughs, chill wind sweeping my hair. Breathing in the scent of dying leaves, fir needles, dark, dank loam, I'd hold it deep in my lungs, exhale it with a song:

"Let there be peace on earth
And let it begin with me.
Let there be peace on earth
The peace that was meant to be.
With God as our father
Brothers all are we;
Let me walk with my brother
In perfect harmony."

That hymn became my wedding song. I hummed it as Mark and I sped on our honeymoon moped. He steered, me hugging his waist, the future stretching before us like the Bermuda roads we traversed—past beaches, railways and marshes, past plantations, forts and stone walls, beneath bougainvilleas and loquats, perfume mixed with salt air.

Eighteen years into our marriage, I remembered that hymn one December evening as I worked. Struggling to meet a deadline, I looked up to rest my eyes, out my office window at the black sky. There I saw lights—strings on the Elliott Bay ferries blinking red, yellow, blue, orange, green. The giant snowflake on the Bon Marché shining over shoppers scurrying the street. Intense green Space Needle beams, the pulsing star on top. Once, seeing that brilliance, I would have sensed God's bond to humankind and the words of the song would have risen, carrying me away. But that night, only anger: What am I doing here? Nothing, let alone peace, will ever begin with me. No one, not even my husband, ever notices me. I have nothing to give, couldn't even make my own babies.

I sighed as I pulled my car into Moshe Ben Maimon's parking lot. I wished I could still feel God's touch the way I had when younger, the way my students still did.

Later, in class that day, with the freshmen settled in their seats, I asked them to take out *Night*. I'd read it in high school myself, the story of Elie Wiesel, a teenage Auschwitz prisoner. Once a child of fervent faith longing to study Kabbalah, he recalls seeing a Gestapo truck dump babies in a flaming pit:

Never shall I forget the little faces of the children, whose bodies I saw turned into wreaths of smoke beneath a silent blue sky.

Never shall I forget those moments which murdered my God and my soul and turned my dreams to dust.

When I'd read those words as a teenager, I cried for Eliezer; how tragic to lose God when you needed him most. When I reread those words as an adult, I cried for myself: Where had my God gone?

"Okay," I said to the freshmen. "Let's open to page sixty-three. We've been talking about how Auschwitz is affecting Eliezer's faith. Sometimes he doesn't believe, as when he sees the burning babies. But sometimes he thanks God, as when he gets to keep his shoes. What happens when the Nazis hang the little boy?" A hand darted up. "Yes, Amira?"

"He has one of those moments when he stops believing in God. But this time, I think it's for good."

"Why?"

"Well, he says while the boy is dying he hears a voice within himself. It whispers God is hanging on the gallows—like God's dying or just doesn't care."

"I think that's right," said Nitza. "Or maybe he's just mad at God. Later, on Rosh Hashanah, he refuses to pray with the prisoners. He never did anything like that before."

"And how does he feel about it?"

Riva flailed a hand. "Oh, I know. Wait. There's a good quote." She leafed through the pages. "Here:

Once, New Year's Day had dominated my life. I knew my sins grieved the Eternal; I implored his forgiveness. Once, I had believed profoundly that upon one solitary deed of mine, one solitary prayer, depended the salvation of the world.

This day I had ceased to plead. My eyes were open and I was

alone—terribly alone in a world without God and without man. Without love or mercy. I had ceased to be anything but ashes. I stood amid that praying congregation, observing it like a stranger."

She looked up, blue eyes piercing me. "Eliezer feels empty and cut off from God."

"He should have prayed and fasted anyway," said Avraham.

"If he doesn't believe in God, wouldn't that be hypocritical?"

Suri shook her head. "No. The Torah says you should do what God tells you even when you don't understand it. It's called *Na'aseh v'nishma.*"

"*Na'as...?*"

"When God wanted to give the Torah, he offered it not only to the Israelites, but to all other nations too. The other nations refused it because the commandments seemed too hard. But when God offered it to the Israelites, they said '*Na'aseh v'nishma*'. We will act and understand."

"That's right," said Channah. "People say that the Jews think they're special because God chose them, but actually they chose God."

Suri nodded. "So, the rabbis tell us you have to do the acts without question and think about them. If you do, you'll learn to understand God. If Eliezer had observed the holidays and thought about them, he might not have felt God didn't care."

Something glass-like shattered in my chest. "What do you mean, think about the acts?"

"Well, you're supposed to read the Torah to understand the acts have meaning, and focus on it when you act."

But I *was* doing the acts. Had always done them, more or less.

That evening I went down into the basement, found the battered *Xmas* box. I plunged my hand through tangled wires and knotted bulb strands—red, multicolored, white—unraveled a string of tiny whites.

We hadn't yet bought a Christmas tree, so I strung them on our family room ficus, plugged in the cord. Bright lights winked at me.

I pulled a dusty Bible from a shelf. In all my years of Catechism, I'd never read one. We'd learned about the deadly sins: lust, gluttony, greed, sloth, wrath, envy, pride, but I knew nothing of the Bible. I opened Genesis:

> In the beginning, when God created the heavens and the earth, the earth was a formless wasteland, and darkness covered the abyss, while a mighty wind swept over the waters. Then God said, "Let there be light," and there was light.

December days slipped by and I tried to think about my actions. Reading the ninth-graders' poems, I aimed to treat each as special, ignore the weight of those remaining in the pile. When I went to Sean's basketball game, I strove to focus on his shots, not the minutes still on the clock. Helping Cristin study history, I tried to listen to her recitations, not wonder what to cook for dinner. When I went to Mark's firm party, I sought to engage in the small talk, not wish to be home in bed. And when I set out the crèche, I tried to think about the Torah.

The Hebrew Scriptures surprised me. No character was perfect, each a faith-flounderer like me. When God promised Abraham a child, the old man laughed in God's face, but then looked deep into the night and saw his children countless as stars. When Jacob dreamed his stairs to Heaven, he thought God was calling him and tried to wrestle God away before stopping, asking to be blessed. When God asked Moses to lead the Exodus, the Hebrew stuttered, claimed to be too feeble. Yet, he parted raging Red Sea waters, Pharaoh's soldiers in fierce pursuit.

On Christmas Eve before Mass, I sat down before my lighted ficus, opened to Malachi:

> See, I will send my messenger, who will prepare the way before me. Then suddenly the Lord you are seeking will come to his

temple; the messenger of the covenant, whom you desire, will come.

That night at Saint James Cathedral, my family slid into a pew. Gilded angels and red poinsettias clustered on polished marble floors. Star lanterns hung from coffered ceilings, velvet banners from pilasters. Fir garlands scenting the air, the ushers rolled in the crèche—Mary smiling, Joseph kneeling, moonfaced Jesus in his crib. And this time, as they entered, I saw something I hadn't seen before, something more than wooden figures: Sean lobbing the basketball to score, scanning the bleachers to see if I was cheering. Cristin biting her pen, smiling as I said "Great job" when she recalled her history dates. Mark introducing me to his partners, eyes gentle, faintly smiling, when I shook their hands. My students picking up their poems, high-fiving and whooping when they saw their grades. And all around, I heard music, buoyant in the cathedral: *For lo! the days are hastening on. . . / When peace shall over all the earth / Its ancient splendors fling / And the whole world send back the song / Which now the angels sing.*

I was silent as Mark drove home from Mass. I looked out the window at the streets—vacant, still—the dark night and countless winking stars.

Sleeping Beauty

October 2003

The classroom door blew open as I packed my briefcase to go home. A cold gust of air rushed in, blowing the papers from my desk, chasing red and gold leaves across the threshold so they swirled and settled at my feet. Kalindah whirled in with the weather. With black-sweatshirted arms, she gave me my daily hug—nubby, slightly dank and fusty—then plopped on the top of a desk, pulling legs akimbo beneath her skirt. "Ms. Vallone, life's so unfair. All my friends have boyfriends but me."

Braces, Janis Joplin hair, Kalindah was a freshman when I first taught at Moshe Ben Maimon. Flicking her chin in Kalindah's direction, Dr. Chernov had warned me about her before her maternity leave. "Make sure you watch out for that one—she's a time bomb waiting to explode, bipolar without her medication. You'll see, one day she'll draw a knife."

During my first yeshiva weeks, Kalindah sat huddled at the back of the classroom, silent, impassive, gray-eyed. Was she sedated? Not till I scheduled a quiz did I see any sign of life. After class she came up to my desk: "I stink at tests." Then she walked out.

Sure enough, her score was 47. When I lay the quiz on her desk, she glanced at the grade, hands stuffed in sweatshirt pouch. "Told you."

I studied the dandruff in her part. "Take it home and do it over. You can use your book and raise your grade."

Metal smile trapping sandwich morsels. "Really? That's awesome!"

I knew Dr. Chernov would not be happy with me.

Tests weren't Kalindah's only problem. For weeks I pumped and prodded: "I'm still waiting for your narrative. Are you planning to turn one in?"

Her response: a shoulder shrug. But one day she came to class early, dropped some rumpled sheets on my desk. "Ms. Vallone, I know it's really late, but I wrote the story."

In the story, the penguin Galápaga wants to cross a river, but she's an orphan, so no one's shown her how. She tries to use her wings as eagles do, but finds them too stubby for flying. She tries to hop across on river rocks, but her legs are too clumsy for leaping. So she uses a fallen tree trunk as bridge between the two banks. But the trunk is very narrow, and it's mossy, high above the water, and though penguins have good gripping toenails, midway across she slips. Plummeting from her perch, she impromptu somersault tucks, plunges in the frigid water, sinks to the bottom. There, she begins to pray: *O God / Fear and trembling come upon me / Oh, that I had wings like a dove! /I would fly away and be at rest.*

Then a strange thing happens. Panic-beating her wings, she rises through the water, discovers she can swim. So she breast strokes across the river, climbs out and waddles toward the woods.

I laughed reading Kalindah's story, wrote *A* at the top, *Great job! In Italian* calinda *means* lark. *So I hope you understand you can fly even though penguins can't!*

Next day when she read my comments, Kalindah smiled and leaped at me, gave me the very first hug.

But what could I say about boys to a girl only sixteen? I gathered the papers from the floor, slipped them into my briefcase, sat on a desk facing Kalindah. "I know it stinks not to have a boyfriend, but someday you'll have one, really. Remember when you thought you couldn't write?"

"Yeah, but I'm not pretty. I wish I could be someone else!"

When I was an adolescent, I wished to be my cousin Angela, three years older than me. *Angela*, the Italian word for *angel*. Angela, who as a child wore the prettiest pinafores, dark hair thickly braided with ribbons. Angela, favored as beautiful, while I was anything but. Aunt Lina said my eyes were beady. The kids at school called me Chinky Girl. Gramma told me I needed a perm, slapped my hands when I bit my nails. Once, in Florence at the Uffizi, my father told me I looked like Titian's *Venus*. As I stared at her dimpled belly and thighs, two British men walked by. "Christ!" one snickered to the other. "Titian? More like tush-man!" And when Dr. Schultz stethoscoped my lungs, he focused on my chest while listening to my breathing, proposed repeated palm-pressing to perk up my flaccid breasts.

In high school, it was Dori Klein I envied, a twin for Zeffirelli's Juliet—chestnut hair tumbling to her waist, blue eyes and dancer's legs. If I were Dori, every evening Michael Goldfarb would scale the lamppost on the corner. He'd peek inside my window as I braided my hair for bed, maybe even whisper to himself: *But, soft! what light through yonder window breaks? / It is the east, and Jan is the sun.*

But as long as Dori was alive, Mike would never look at me. Nor would Gary, nor Mitchell, nor Jeff.

It's not that I came from bad stock. My mother, like hers, had curly hair, twinkling eyes, a heart-shaped face. And oh what a figure in the photo, bathing-suited at age sixteen, a Sophia Loren on a rock, sunning at Kaaterskill Falls. So it was for my Aunt Marie, my cousins Marianne and Celeste. Of all the females in my family, only I lacked the magic genes.

I remember when I was sixteen. Angela sat me on the pink counter of our grandmother's tiny bathroom, my back towards the mirror, legs dangling. She pushed my hair behind my ears, perused my face with her kohled golden eyes. Bubbling in her Brooklyn brogue, she broke into a glossy smile, "I've got it!"

She unzipped her floral makeup bag with a flick of her bracelet-trimmed wrist. Out came a bottle of foundation muddying up my face.

Out came a tin of eye-shadow blizzarding blue my lids. Out came a mascara spiral coating my lashes black. Out came a sparkling swivel-stick staining my lips cherry red.

When she was finished, Angela stepped back. She lifted my face with a finger, turned it right and left, called, "Gramma, come see!"

Pots clanging in the kitchen, pitter-patters up the hall. Gramma squeezed into the bathroom, squinted at my face. She nodded, "Much bedda."

My heart bloomed a rose.

Then Angela stirred her fingers in her makeup bag, pulled out a rhinestone-trimmed mirror. "Okay—now you can see."

She held the mirror before me. But Juliet wasn't reflected there. Instead, I saw a clown.

In my twenties, it was Holly Brown I longed to be. She was a graduate student when I lab-teched at U.N.C. Every morning she'd sashay to her bench, flicking her Farrah Fawcett mane: "Good mornin' y'all." And as jasmine gardenia perfume gusted from her curly halo, the male med techs would look up from their microscopes, dropping jaws to gawk. In my corner, I'd reach for the radio, turn up the volume of Bruce Springsteen: *Show a little faith there's magic in the night / You ain't a beauty but hey you're alright.*

But I wasn't all right. So I spent a few days' salary to reinvent myself as Holly. As I sat before a salon mirror, Jean Paul pumped the swivel chair, raising the object of his art. He shampooed my hair in awapuhi—wafting ginger scent—parted it into sections, paper-wrapped each around a rod. He squeezed on glycerol monothioglycolate, plastic-capped my head. He helmeted me with a dryer and toggled on the heat. My scalp prickled and crawled. My ears sizzled like bacon. But the dryer drone fired my fantasies as I flipped through a *Vogue* on Brooke Shields: Maybe the lab crew will realize I'm a dove and Holly's a crow.

Maybe Mark will marry me.

Jean Paul rinsed my head to stop the process. He cut and blew dry my hair. Then he swiveled my chair towards the mirror—voilà: Christ, I have a fro.

Mark teased at me when he saw it. He grabbed his camera from the closet, clicked as I pillow-wrapped my head, then hugged me when I burst out crying, said he loved me anyway. For a month I applied Frizz Ease, wore a hat, refused to go out. As soon as an inch of new hair grew, I switched stylists, got a tomboy cut.

I'm embarrassed to admit that in my thirties, my desire was to look like Princess Di—the ultra-toned body, bright smile, the sassy short hair. The lash-brushing coquette bangs, the rose-petal royal British skin. So I went to aerobics, tried Pearl Drops, washed my face with Clinique, and the Christmas my sister Pat visited I had my hair cut Diana style.

When Pat arrived with her family, my niece Kimberly, age five, leaped into my arms. I kissed her cheek, smoothed loose tendrils from her forehead, noticed a crop of drying scabs. I looked at Pat, raised my brows.

"Oh, she's getting over the chickenpox. But she's not contagious anymore."

I'd never had the chickenpox. Two weeks later I saw the first spot. Within days I was covered with pox, then pox^2, pox^3, pox^4. When they healed, they left scars on my chin; every mirror made me turn away. The marks seemed to shout from my jaw, "Hey, see how repulsive she is!" And whenever I had a conversation, the other person seemed transfixed by my chin.

What would Princess Diana do about such horrid imperfections?

I made an appointment with Dr. Fleisch, a Seattle dermatologist. He told me the fix was dermabrasion. If I elected the surgery, he'd give me medication to relax. Then he'd cleanse my face with antiseptic, apply a spray to insta-freeze my skin. That done, he'd use a rotary tool to sand off several epidermal layers. Post-op, the site would be raw, requiring pain relievers. My face would take three months to heal, need sun-shields for six to eight. Luckily, side effects were few—infections, fever blisters, scars, thickened skin, splotchy pigmentation.

I squirmed as Dr. Fleisch disclosed the details, chin skin stinging as he spoke. I asked if many patients chose the surgery.

"It's a commoner procedure."

So I knew that Di would never do it; I'd have to research something else.

Why should physical beauty be the object of lifelong yearning? Trigger decades of envy and grief? Prompt cosmetics, surgery, false hope? And why, even into my forties, did I still pine to be a dove among the crows? How I fussed on a trip to Palermo before visiting my step-grandmother. The last time I'd seen Mimma, I was barely into my twenties. Now she was eighty-six, I a wife, the mother of two teens. Still, I slathered my wrinkles with creams, bleached my teeth, tinted my hair. I asked Cristin to help me choose my clothes—Capris to mask my thighs, long sleeves to hide my arms. And what did Mimma do when Mark showed her the Polaroid he'd taken after she'd scaled two flights like a jilly-goat to fetch her brother for lunch? After she served us a four-course meal she'd cooked and served herself? After she toured us around the apartment she still dusted, swept and mopped? She shook her head at the photo and covered her image with her hand. "*O Dio*, I old."

A short walk from Mimma's apartment is the Convento dei Cappuccini. In 1599 the monks noticed something strange: their catacombs released mysterious vapors that mummified the dead. When the monks announced the discovery, they set off a public frenzy. People clamored to be buried there to preserve their beauty after death.

In the catacombs' long dank corridors rest eight thousand catalogued corpses. Men are grouped and labeled by profession—priests, lawyers, soldiers, professors, writers, doctors—women by their state of womb—virgins, barren wives, mothers. Each is suspended by the neck like a lamb hanging at the butcher's, each wearing Sunday's best clothes. A monk hovers in a cassock, penance rope around his neck. A woman wafts hoop-skirted, wielding a parasol. A soldier sentries in uniform and a wide three-cornered hat.

There's a special section for children. The last catacombed corpse was a girl who died of croup in 1920. Frocked flouncily in pink, ringlets gathered in a bow, she rests in a transparent casket. The monks call her Sleeping Beauty, but there's little beauty in the crypt. Sleeping Beauty's skin is doll-waxy, her hair faded, dull, limp. And the flesh of the corpses around her is either mummified or gone. Many faces grimace, some mouthing Edvard Munch screams, the husks of their decaying bodies coated with decades of dust.

But I couldn't tell Kalindah about the catacombs. Or that Dori went skating with her boyfriend on a lake near her college dorm and drowned falling through the ice. Or that Angela discovered stage-three cancer and lost her breasts and hair. Or that my mother developed a neuroma that twisted and paralyzed her face. Or that Prince Charles divorced Diana, who died in a car crash shortly after. Or that when I thought about the women whose beauty I envied all my life, I closed my eyes and thanked God for my wrinkles.

Instead, I pulled a snapshot from my wallet—my family in the Umbrian sun. "Kalindah, you're fine just as you are. Look, let me show you something. These are the people I love most in the world: Mark—we've been married twenty-three years. Cristin—she's your age. Sean, who's two years younger. And Kalindah, when I was sixteen, I didn't know a single one of them."

Kalindah took the photo from my hands. She studied it a moment, looked up. "Your daughter's really pretty. She looks a lot like you."

Hot Sox

December 2006

I lay in bed curled like a fetus, blankets pulled over my head to
seal out the morning light. Burning brow, frozen feet, leaden
limbs. Normally, I would have rolled out of bed, taken some
DayQuil, put on warm socks and trod off to work nonetheless. I hated
missing school. But today I would call in sick, because it was more than
my body that ailed me. Once again I was questioning my competence,
my ability to be a good teacher.

I burrowed more deeply in my sheets. Just picturing myself in the
classroom was a blade piercing the heart—September, the first day of
school, juniors looking me over, rain rapping on the roof. "Hi everyone,"
I say. "I'm Ms. Vallone, and this is my candle." I strike a match and touch it
to the wick, watch the flame gasp and struggle for life. "I light it every time
I welcome a new group of students to remind us why we're here. During
this semester, I plan to teach you everything I know about writing, and I
hope in the future, you'll write to make a difference in the world—take
my tiny flame, add it to yours, use it to light the flames of others."

I winced. Do I even *have* a flame? Who am I to teach writing?

Sure, as a student, I'd written dozens of papers, and thousands of
memos and contracts in the course of my law career. But people often
scoffed at legalese.

Said Kafka: "A lawyer is a person who writes a ten thousand-word
document and calls it *a brief*." And Will Rogers: "The minute you read
something that you can't understand, you can almost be sure that it
was drawn up by a lawyer."

Strange, but when I started teaching, I felt confident about my
writing. I'd always loved to do it, been told I did it well. In third-

grade, Mrs. Gold stood up from her desk one day. She reached for the classroom flag, slid the dowel from its berth above the board. Carefully she rolled it, tied it with ribbon and bow, motions that always hushed the class. "Tomorrow is Lincoln's birthday, so it's time for another Flag Award." I watched as she sashayed down the U, V, W row, expected one more Karen Wilde award (Rhinoceros. R-H-I-N-O-C-E-R-O-S. Rhinoceros.) But Mrs. Gold stopped promenading prematurely, pointed the flag into my hand. "This is for your excellent poem on my favorite president. Lincoln loved to write. May you always follow his example. Tomorrow, fly this flag with pride."

Pride. I felt it in sixth grade too, when Mr. Bonners chose my peace essay as a time capsule artifact. At the all-school assembly, the breeze ruffled my hair as the boys rolled the capsule to the hole they'd dug in the schoolyard. The capsule thudded to the bottom, then the swish of shovels in dry dirt, the ping of pebbles on steel. The capsule would be unearthed three decades later, in the year 2000, when my essay would be read to a generation who'd never known war. In eighth grade, I was proud once more when I entered a limerick contest sponsored by the American Dental Association. My poem took first prize and became a brush-your-teeth jingle on Nassau County radio.

When it came to writing, not even adulthood set me straight. Georgetown's Dr. Singh called my application essay *art.* N.Y.U.'s Professor Rosen gave me Honors in Legal Writing. And Primo Inc.'s C.E.O. Dick Krass, said my contracts were the best he'd ever read.

Yes, it was true: I could write if nothing else. Writing was written in my genes, a gift from my *raconteur* father, who even died with a tale upon his lips. Seventy, recently retired, in critical care with lymphoma, he'd Dictaphoned a memoir about his Uncle Mario for his writing class.

He'd also instructed me well: Never write without a dictionary. Learn every word you read. Use every word precisely. Keep a grammar book on your desk. Over and over and over, he recounted one of his cases, a million-dollar lawsuit that turned on one comma placement. I still imagine the scene—disorder in the courtroom, the judge pounding gavel on bench, my father's words:

"Your Honor, as you know, this dispute began when Mr. Schved notified Mr. Bernstein that he was canceling an easement agreement governing Mr. Schved's use of Mr. Bernstein's land. The relevant provision is as follows:

> This agreement shall be effective from the date it is made and shall continue in force for a period of ten (10) years from the date it is made, and thereafter for successive ten (10) year terms, unless and until terminated by one year's prior written notice by either party.

"Mr. Bernstein argues that the easement runs for a full ten years, even though Mr. Schved gave notice to cancel in year three. He claims damages of one million dollars, the present value of seven years' payments.

"Mr. Bernstein, however, errs. He misconstrues the single sentence that comprises said provision. Said sentence contains three clauses, separated by two commas, which I shall refer to as Clauses One through Three and Commas One and Two. Pursuant to the rule of antecedent clauses set forth in *Warriner's Grammar*, said sentence denotes that the termination notice is applicable to *both* the initial ten-year term *and* each successive term. Specifically, Comma Two signifies that Clause Three pertains to both antecedent clauses, that is, Clause One *and* Clause Two, not just to the latter, Clause Two, as Mr. Bernstein contends. Therefore, Mr. Schved was entitled to cancel the contract at any time during the initial term *or* any renewal term, *not* just during a renewal term, upon one year's notice to Bernstein."

The judge is silent a moment, the crowd's eyes fixed on him. He nods. "Ladies, gentlemen, counselors, this court holds in favor of Mr. Schved."

So my father never ceased reminding me: "A comma can be worth a million dollars."

And I had other teachers. Afternoons my mother advised me on homework as I wrote at the kitchen table. She would stand behind the counter cutting dough cords into *gnocchi*, urging me to read my words aloud. Her response to a choppy sentence: "You need to make more music!" Her retort to a lackluster passage: "Paint pictures with your words!"

Then there was Ralph, a senior partner at Malkovich Fein. When I was still a young lawyer, he summoned me to his office, asked me to draft a lease, tendered a standardized form. But before I could ask any questions, his phone began to ring, so he motioned me into a chair. He smacked the speaker button on, nattered at length with a client, smacked the speaker button off, buzzed his secretary in. When she arrived, he grabbed a copy of the lease form. Gunning through the pages, he struck provisions with a pen and dictated new ones to his secretary, General Patton mode. When she left, he turned to me. I poised my pen on my notepad, but Ralph waved me out of his office. "Never be strangled by forms."

So, when I started teaching, I assuredly counseled my students, "When you write, details make a difference. Make music and paint pictures with your words. Never censor your voice. And revise, revise, revise."

Zach did exactly as I said. During his senior year, he wrote a memoir about his brother who'd died from a brain glioma. He followed my comments on structure, my recommendations on voice. He asked me for help with word choices, purged every comma splice. He revised, met me for feedback, revised, came back for more.

I submitted the memoir to a contest sponsored by *Polaris*—stories of motivation and faith, most by Protestant writers from the South and Midwest. A wedding gift from Mark's mother, she renewed my subscription each Christmas, a sign of her faith I'd someday ditch John Paul II for John Calvin. And I had faith the magazine editor would note a motivated Jewish boy.

Entering my house some months later, I dropped my keys on the counter, saw the phone light blinking, pushed it. "This is Frank Linham from *Polaris*. Your student Zach has placed second in our contest. He's won a sizable scholarship and will be published in our magazine."

Zach's parents asked me over for Shabbat. That Friday just before sunset, his mother had lit the Sabbath candles, one for each member of her family, three fanning motions per flame, then rested her hands on her eyelids to draw the light to her. By the time Mark and I arrived, the dining room glowed like a chapel. We sat down at the table, where Zach's father blessed his children, us, the wine, the bread:

"*Barukh atah Adonai Elohaynu melekh ha-olam Kiy vanu vacharta v'otanu qidashta mikol ha'amiym.*" "Blessed are You, Lord, our God, King of the Universe. You have chosen us for Your service, and given us a sacred purpose in life."

Then Zach's mother served the Sabbath feast. *Challah*, chicken soup, matzoh balls. Potato kugel, gefilte fish, salad. Beef brisket, apple cake, brownies.

After dinner, Zach handed me a box. Resting it on the table, I removed the lid, untucked the tissue paper. Inside was a crystal candelabra blown of purple-violet, two necks, each for one candle, entwined like mating swans.

Precious, so precious, the only trophy of my life. I placed it on a ledge at home where sun streaming through the windows flecked purple-violet on the walls.

That's when it began. *Polaris* became to me what Kelley Drye had been to my father: an Oz I'd never reach, to which I'd guided someone else. But rather than scorn it as my father had, I sought to attain it for myself. I emailed Frank Linham a story I'd written about adoption. It was thoughtful and moving, the kind he'd leap to publish, oozing drive and faith. After all, wasn't my writing light-years better than that of the farmers who filled his magazine? And hadn't I been the one who taught Zach everything he knew?

Jan,

> This story is very interesting and well told. But it's not focused enough for a *Polaris* story. Fertility stories are also common enough. Pick a more unusual topic. Maybe you have an interfaith story about being an Xian teaching at a yeshiva. Or maybe you have a friend's story you'd like to ghost-write?

Yours truly,

Frank

So I wrote a yeshiva story.

Jan,

> This story is indeed interesting. The problem is that you are the hero of the story. You're not the learner. Yes, there is that memory of being excluded, but the overall message is about what you can do as a teacher for these kids. Maybe that's the inherent problem with this narrative. It just doesn't work as a *Polaris* narrative.

I pitched it and wrote about my jewelry theft.

Jan,

> Not enough story here. It's more of a devotional. The family as the heirloom jewels is a nice touch, but it's soft and doesn't have enough narrative to make a full *Polaris* story.

> Here are some areas of need for us. We're always looking for Horn of Plenty stories. Got a recipe that has a story connected to it (and the story is the important part)? Preferably not a dessert recipe. We've got lots of those.

Oh, how I cried. I pictured Frank in his New York office, high over the rainbow, punching buttons, pulling levers, and myself aground in Emerald City, searching for a wizard who'd wave his magic wand. Why didn't he notice my talent, my courage, perseverance? Why couldn't he see my enthusiasm, dedication, smarts? Come on Frank, just a page! One bitsy page in your magazine! Frank, please tell me why *if happy little bluebirds fly beyond the rainbow, why oh why can't I?*

He wants me to write about lasagna?

Instead, I made some. I invited my closest friends for dinner to make myself feel talented, loved. I wheeled my cart around Whole Foods, chose tomatoes, imported curly noodles, hand-made pork Italian sausage. I selected the freshest local basil, ricotta and mozzarella. Only extra-virgin for my pantry. Only fine Sicilian salt. Arranging odd layers lengthwise, setting the evens across, I stacked it six inches high. A *capolavoro* lasagna. I ironed our best linen tablecloth, the one with the grapevine motif, set out our dishes from Deruta, polished the silverware. I removed two twelve-inch tapers from a box. Then I reached standing on tip-toes for my candelabra on its shelf. Right ankle twisting, giving way. Purple shards scattered on the floor.

Once, I watched a young contestant on American Idol. Long, gleaming black hair, smiling red flamenco lips, she led the camera through her father's *taqueria,* pointing to trophies on a shelf. "I've been singing all my life. My teacher says God's given me a gift."

Then she stood before judges, Rolexed Randy, cleavaged Paula, white-toothed Simon. "I'm here to be the next Idol. I'll be singing Whitney Houston." Chin and hands rising, she began to sing: "*I believe that children are our future / Teach them well and let them lead the way / Show them all the beauty they possess inside.*"

Randy tapped his pen. Paula bit her lips. Just as the singer finished, Simon leaned back in his seat: "Sorry, Darling, your singing teacher lied."

The singer scanned the threesome, gun-barreled a long red nail at Simon. "*Él es un coger loco! COGER LOCO!*"

A bouncer escorted her out the door.

Once I read a psychology book on the human mind. It said the brain is naturally programmed to protect our self-esteem. It emphasizes self-aggrandizing memories, ignores recollections that disgrace.

Oh, *pobrecita*, I am you.

After my exchanges with the wizard, I bought *The Situation and the Story, The Art of Writing Memoir, Crafting a Life in Essay, Story Poem.* I read them like a chain smoker dragging Dunhills, then enrolled in a summer writing program at the Bread Loaf School, Vermont. For six weeks I lived without my family, sitting quasi-lotus on a dorm bed, pillow my iBook desk. I typed and typed and typed. I revised, revised, revised. I swatted mosquitoes with a notepad, sweat trickling down my back in the humid Green Mountain heat. My first paper was a magnum opus submitted one Monday in July:

> Most of us need to feel loved—loved by our parents, loved by our friends, loved by our lovers and children. Love provides us with us a reason to live and the strength to carry on when life becomes difficult. Love, however, is intangible; it cannot be touched or seen. It is not always clear that we have found it, so we search for evidence of love. A smile, a hug, a card or a token might provide us with evidence of love, and whenever love's evidence comes our way, we hold on to it with all of our might. We memorize the shape and gleam of the smile and the warmth and scent of the hug, and we place the card or the token in a special memory box. Evidence of love can sustain us, because it proves to us that we are loved.

At week's end, I sat in the circle of desks arranged around the classroom. Professor Véreux, an aging Clint Eastwood, crepe-soled the hardwood floor. Without a word, he dropped a paper on each desk. I looked up as he loosed my essay, sunlight hazing him a specter. My paper slid across the desk. I caught it before it skated off.

Stapled to the front of it was an extra sheet, a conceptual three-D plan of metal building girders bolted at ninety-degrees, a short note beneath:

> Your inclination is to be somewhat overly-structured, which has the upside of thoroughness and a downside of rigidity and tediousness. You should make it a goal to learn how to use that inclination without becoming so locked into it that you can't be imaginative.

A seaweed sensation in my stomach. I'd written the paper from my heart. How could he find it tedious? I'd done my best to make my words Monets. How had they turned out Venus Paradise?

For the next few weeks I barely rested. Each night, I wrote till after midnight, straining to exhume my dead right brain. One night, I submitted to exhaustion, turned out the lights, crawled in my narrow bed. Nuzzling into the pillow, I closed my eyes.

Buzz.

Damn these Vermont bugs. I rolled over, wrapped my pillow round my head.

Buzz, buzz.

Please go away.

Buzz, buzz, buzz.

I sat up in the dark. High on the wall, a tiny green beacon.

Slipping out of bed, I picked up a folder from the floor, sighted my target, readied like a Stealth. I flailed the folder at the firefly:

Whoosh, buzz, whoosh, buzz, whoosh.

Silence. A trickle of neck sweat. I scoped the room—green flicker on the dresser. Holding my breath, I picked up an empty water glass, turned it upside down, raised it overhead. Thwack. I trapped the bug.

Take that, Véreux. Take that.

Green-flashing-ricochet in glass.

• • • • •

I'd been working on a memoir about a teaching breakthrough I'd had with my student Kalindah. Following class, a few days after I'd turned it in, Véreux pulled me aside. "We need to talk in The Barn."

I followed him out of the classroom, trailed him like a geisha across the lawn. Here and there students read on pastel Adirondacks—blue, yellow, pink or green. Holding *Faerie Queenes* overhead, they shielded their eyes against the sun. Voices carried from the clapboard theater, doors propped open in the heat: *Why, man, he doth bestride the narrow world / Like a Colossus, and we petty men / Walk under his huge legs and peep about. . . / The fault, dear Brutus, is not in our stars / But in ourselves, that we are underlings.*

When Véreux reached The Barn, I followed him into its shuttered shadows. Wicker chairs were scattered here and there in coffee odor mugginess. Véreux motioned me to a wicker. I sat clasping my laptop to my chest.

He took a chair, leaned toward me. "I can't accept your story."

My gut, seaweedy, faint. "Excuse me?"

"I'm returning your memoir. The ending is dishonest. That moment with your student—it's saccharine. And what you said to her—a teacher should never say that."

My throat, choking kelp. "I described what I felt."

He dropped the story on my lap. "Don't be obstinate. You have two choices—rewrite it or discard it." He stood and left the room.

Why do so many people view cynicism as wisdom, joy as foolishness? Take a walk in the city; misery is easy to see—the wild-haired homeless man who sits on a fruit crate on Roosevelt. He plies his cardboard sign: *Viet Nam vet will work.* The tube-topped teen who prowls Aurora North at night. She raps on cars stopped at red lights: "Hey, you wanna blow job?" Doesn't it take more insight to sieve life for moments of wonder, sift sand for mother-of-pearl? Still, I invented a new ending for my story, went for bitter irony. And despite Véreux's dismissiveness—or maybe on account of it—my heart quavered when his comments arrived:

> The last section of this story is a big improvement over the earlier
> version, and I'll accept it as your last paper and give it a grade of
> A. I think you have the skills to become a fine personal essayist.

I re-read his judgment several times. *Fine*. Did that mean *good*? Somehow it suggested *bad*. And what did he mean by *skills*? It implied something less than *talent*. As for the *A* on my fiction—another fabulous fake.

Sometimes I think I became a teacher to counterbalance the Véreuxs of the world. That I left my job at law to make it my job to say *good job* to others. What had Véreux's teachers said to him in school? Did Véreux disparage his students to avenge his own teachers' slights? Did people like Véreux sense that giving praise diminished their stash? Or was withholding it a simple power trip? And why did I even care what people like Véreux thought of me? Why did I let these rocks in my garden to become my father and god? Was I trying to extract from them what I couldn't chisel from the dead? Why didn't I kick them from the bed?

Instead, I kicked off my blankets, sneezed, shivered up my spine. Damn. I'm a terrible writer. I was better as a lawyer. I'll never do that candle thing again.

I rolled out of bed. Pulling on a robe, I headed to the porch to fetch the paper. There I saw something wedged in the knocker of the door. I dislodged it: a brand new pair of socks with a holographic tag glittering like diamonds. Hot Sox. I unrolled them. Black cotton patterned with menorahs and gilt-thread candle flames. A gift from one of my students? I would never know. I slipped them on my feet. Then I dressed, took some Dayquil, went to school.

Part III

If I speak in human and angelic tongues but do not have love, I am a resounding gong or a clashing cymbal.

And. . .if I have all faith so as to move mountains but do not have love, I am nothing.

If I give away everything I own. . .so that I may boast but do not have love, I gain nothing.

Love is patient, love is kind. It is not jealous, is not pompous, it is not inflated. . .it does not brood over injury. . .but rejoices with the truth.

It bears all things, believes all things, hopes all things, endures all things.

—1 Corinthians 13: 1-7

• • • • •

Rabbi Yochanan the Sandal-Maker would say: Every gathering that is for the sake of Heaven will last forever; that is not for the sake of Heaven will not last.

—Pirkei Avot: 4.11

The Story of the Cave

July 1999

Our car coursed down the highway that runs south along Sicily's western coast. Mark, intently driving, nodded his head to Radio Italia, and Cristin and Sean, not quite teenagers, slumped in the backseat, asleep. I gazed out the window of the car, the sky a metallic blue lid, the sun a blazing orange disc, the asphalt a molten black strip. To my right, the Mediterranean sparkled and craggy cliffs jutted out from blond sand. Intermittently, we passed a populated area: here a pristine medieval town with church towers and parapets, there a sprawl of squalid houses with corrugated metal roofs. It wasn't quite like I'd imagined. Italy is famous for preserving the past; yet much of Sicily was rundown.

I ticked off the signposts we drove by: Palermo, Castellammare, Alcamo. "Mark, how much longer?"

He cast me a sideways glance, my face reflecting in his sunglasses. "Well, Segesta should be next, Castelvetrano right after that."

I looked back out the window, but no longer saw the scenery outside. Instead, I saw my mother in her hospital bed, as she'd been two months earlier, the last time we spoke before she died. She'd not been as lucky as Mark, whose cancer had been cured. She had lived with breast cancer for over five years. Body thin and frail, she slept.

I bent down over her ear. "Mom, can you hear me?"

She started, eyes wild, gaped about her in an arc, as if trying to fathom where she was. When she spotted me, her eyes latched mine and she clutched my hand. "I saw Papa and Mama."

Her parents had long been dead. I studied my mother's face—frightened, bewildered—as my face must had been when Sister Clara first taught about death. She told us seven-year-olds that Heaven is a house with many rooms, one for each of us. All during our lives, God prepares our places, and when we die our dead loved ones will come to take us there. Had my mother learned the same? A shiver snaked up my spine. "That sounds nice, Mom. What were they doing?"

Like a child refusing broccoli, she shook her head from side to side. "They called and reached for me, but I don't want to go." She pursed her lips. "I also saw your father. But he pushed me away."

And that's exactly where I looked, for her eyes were asking me why. Why had my father left her after twenty-four years of marriage? What had he seen in Carol that he hadn't seen in her? Why hadn't he loved her?

My mother squeezed my hand. "But Papa loves Mama."

All through their lives, my grandparents personified love. My grandfather ogled my grandmother as if she were Sophia Loren, long after she lost her figure, long after her hair grayed and thinned. And my grandmother doted on my grandfather. Each morning she laid out the suit and shirt she'd ironed for him, each evening she served him *carne* and each night she fluffed his armchair cushions so he could watch T.V. Tuesdays they came to Baldwin bearing Perugina candies, Thursdays they played Bingo at the Knights of Columbus Hall, and every year they sailed the *da Vinci* to visit Castelvetrano. In our family, theirs was a legendary love story.

My cousin Marianne first told me their story when I was twelve years old, a lovelorn adolescent; Michael Goldfarb wouldn't look at me. One Sunday evening, we conferred in the back bedroom of our grandparents' Brooklyn rowhouse as our family played poker, cracked chestnuts and quaffed espresso around the kitchen table. They thwacked their cards on the table, told jokes (What kind of fun does a priest have? Nun.), rued the Democratic gaps (missile and credibility), professed enduring *like* for Ike and Abraham Lincoln. My grandfather, as always, presided over his court seated at the head of the table with my grandmother at his side, their hands holding up wide fans of cards, elbows lightly touching on the Formica.

In spite of the din in the kitchen, my cousin spoke softly. "Don't worry. One day, you'll find love, and when you do, it will last forever."

I had every reason to believe her; Marianne was six years older and would know. Still, I pressed: "How can you be sure?"

She glanced at herself in a mirror, twisting her long chestnut hair and pinning it on top of her head. "Well, look at Gramma and Grampa."

According to Marianne, my grandfather was smitten by my grandmother the moment he first saw her. Short, rigid and barrel-chested, with the olive-skin, thick black hair and espresso eyes of most Sicilians, he was not an attractive young man. Nor was he rich. The first of six sons, he'd been born to a family of *contadini* in the scorched, dusty village of Castelvetrano. His parents had named him Paolo, meaning *small and humble.* So small and humble was my grandfather, that when my grandmother agreed to marry him, he praised the Virgin Mary on his knees. My grandmother was apparently quite a catch. Petite, pliant and poised, with strawberry-blond hair and smiling blue eyes that distinguished her from the other Castelvetranan girls, she was considered a great beauty. She was also a *contessa*, the descendant of Sicilian patricians. Her parents had named her Celeste, meaning *heavenly.*

As my cousin told me the story, I stared at the antique clock that sat on my grandfather's desk in the corner of the bedroom. For as long as I could remember, it hadn't worked, hands fixed at seven thirteen. Yet somehow, I could see my grandparents' youth reflected in its crystal, where it took on more detail and color than my cousin's words supplied. Paolo, a sun-bronzed boy running rampant with a troop of younger brothers, all of them shirtless and shoeless, raising dust and spooking chickens in a farmyard. Celeste, a lemon-frocked girl, pony trotting down a hillside, tresses floating on the breeze, glinting riding boots. Paolo, a brooding adolescent, toiling with his parents in an orchard, plucking olives from a twisted tree, eking out a living from the land. Celeste, a bright and buoyant teen, lounging on the terrace of a villa, sipping orange soda with her girlfriends, giggling in rose bower shade.

Marianne never told me how my grandparents met. Before she could finish her tale, my parents peeked into the room to tell me it was time to leave. So during the car ride home, I stared out the backseat window, completing the story myself, embellishing the scene, screening it on the dark night sky.

Inside a village church in Castelvetrano, candles glow, a vigil Mass. A priest in bright white vestments consecrates Communion wafers and wine, raises a disc and chalice heavenward:

Breaking the wafer in two, he beckons the parishioners to receive it. The people in the front pews rise, turn towards the center aisle, begin to process to the altar. Among them is Celeste. She's maybe sixteen, hands clasped, lace veiling bowed head. From a back pew Paolo spots her. *O! So shows a snowy dove trooping with crows, / As yonder lady o'er her fellows shows / Did my heart love till now? Forswear it, sight! / For I ne'er saw true beauty till this night.* As if drawn by a mystical power, Celeste turns precisely at that moment, notices Paolo and smiles.

Today, I keep a sepia wedding photograph in my living room. My grandfather looks out from the picture, chest swelling, mustache-tips sharp, a Victor Emanuel. No longer small and humble, he wears a tuxedo, rose in the buttonhole, handkerchief in the breast pocket. His shirt is communion wafer crisp, his bowtie onyx black. My grandmother stands beside him smiling like Mona Lisa, bobbed hair curling at her cheeks. Her beaded gown plunges at the neckline flaunting flapper fringes and her crescent moon hat sprays gauzy lace from each down-turned tip. The pair hold a rose cascade jointly in their hands, and they float on the heavenly clouds of the photo's airbrushed edge.

And float is exactly what they did. My grandparents Errante, a surname meaning *wanderers*, steam-shipped to America, to them the Promised Land. One spring Mark and I took our children aboard an Ellis Island ferry to research my grandparents' immigration. As the boat entered New York Harbor, I pictured the century-old scene, before the Empire State Building, before the World Trade Center. Ship anchors sliding into silt, whistles shrilling, Paolo takes Celeste by the hand, and they clamber up steerage deck steps, pressing through the roiling crowd: *Eccoci! Hier sind wir! Evo nas! Aquí estamos! Nous voici!* They make their way to the main deck, wide-eyed gaze around. The harbor teems with tugboats, Manhattan monoliths rising. Shielding his eyes from the sun, Paolo looks across the Hudson. He points: "*Guarda,* Celeste!" Lady Liberty, copper clad, salt-green, thrusts her torch in the sky.

After docking at Ellis Island, we entered the turreted Main Building, where immigrants had been received and processed. On the lobby walls hung huge black-and-white photographs of turn-of-the-century immigrants. I wandered among them like a nomad, paused before a young Sicilian couple standing on the dock—a light-haired, long skirted woman with a large-buttoned, boiled-wool jacket. A sharp-mustached, dark-coated man in a bright white shirt.

Walking through the building, I imagined my grandparents' reception—pushing through the crowded Baggage Room, eager to reclaim their trunks. Spiraling upstairs as health officials tagged the lame for deportation. Pressing through the barrel-vaulted Registry Room, where doctors buttonhooked eyelids to quarantine trachoma victims. Entering the "Place of Babel," where stiff-collared bureaucrats probed arrivals for moral fitness.

Later in the day, we searched the Ellis Island immigration records. Hunched before a carreled P.C., my family crowding around me, I typed *Errante* and scrolled the emerging list: Anna Errante, Dante Errante, Emilio Errante, Francesco Errante, Gaspare Errante, Maria Errante, Niccolo Errante, Olimpia Errante, Paolo Errante.

Seeing my grandfather's name, I thrilled as Columbus must have when he first saw the New World's pink horizon. "Look, he's here!"

Mark leaned over my shoulder. "Well, what do you know. Paolo Errante, Castelvetrano. Arrived 1909, age eleven."

I turned back to the screen. "Eleven? But, I thought they were married. . . And where's my grandmother, anyway? She should be between Anna and Dante."

"Do you know her maiden name?"

Fumbling, I typed Celeste Cusa. "Here she is—Castelvetrano. Arrived 1904, age 4."

Mark patted my head. "Well, it made a good story."

Not long after I saw Marianne, I sat propped on my bed with *Wuthering Heights,* my heart beating fast. Heathcliffe was describing how the death of his true love Catherine was affecting him. *That, which you may suppose the most potent to arrest my imagination, is actually the least: for what is not connected with her to me? and what does not recall her?*

The phone rang in the kitchen. I ignored it, tucked my hair behind my ear. *I cannot look down to this floor, but her features are shaped in the flags! In every cloud, in every tree—filling the air at night, and caught by glimpses in every object by day.*

My mother's voice murmured in the background. I flipped the page. *I am surrounded with her image! The most ordinary faces of men and women—my own features—mock me with a resemblance.*

Footsteps up the stairs. *The entire world is a dreadful collection of memoranda that she did exist, and that I have lost her!*

Tapping on my bedroom door. My mother poked in her head, eyes blinking tears. "Honey, may I come in? Gramma died this morning."

After the funeral, my grandfather moved into our house. He no longer condemned Lyndon Johnson, praised Lincoln or told Sicilian tales. He no longer swooped Pat and me to Nunley's (to him, *The Nunnery*) to ride the brass-ringed carousel. He rarely came out of his bedroom, no longer dressed in a suit. He paced the floor at night. My mother worried, whispered with my father. Pat and I shrank from his eyes.

One morning, about a year after my grandmother died, my parents, Pat and I were breakfasting in the kitchen. It was springtime, the window open, a crabapple sharing its scent. My mother poured my father coffee. "I'm not sure what to do. One of my students lost his coat, and the weather's so co—."

The stairs up the hall creaked. Silent, all of us turned.

My grandfather entered the kitchen. He was wearing a suit and fresh shirt, hair Brylcreemed and combed. He took a chair, slapped his hands on the table, rattling the coffee pot and cups. "I've booked a passage to Palermo. The *da Vinci* leaves next week. I'll stay with my cousin in Castelvetrano." Then he helped himself to some espresso, stirred in sugar and swigged it down.

Months later, I was doing homework in the kitchen when my mother brought in the mail. Thumbing through the envelopes, she removed one from the pile, perused it front and back. Made of lightweight paper, its red and blue border signaled airmail, its winged-white-horse stamp *italiano*. My mother slit it open, revealing its light-blue lining, and pulled out a color Polaroid now glued in my family photo album. In the snapshot, my grandfather smiles under a cloudless sky, to his left a strapping staked sapling, to his right a pink stone grotto. The grotto is large enough to enter. Inside, a niched haloed Madonna prays over a small marble table. Outside, a porcelain photo of my grandmother is affixed to the rock above a plaque.

My mother handed me the picture, turned the envelope upside down, and a diaphanous slip of paper fell to the floor. She picked it up and read to me: "Dear Josephine—This is Mama's grotto. It is located in a very prestigious place in Castelvetrano, outside the hospital." She smiled. "Papa loves Mama."

Thirty-two years later, my mother's head nestled in her pillow, eyes fluttering closed. Her grip on my hand loosened, tremoring my heart, but her chest beneath the covers maintained its rise and fall.

"Mom?"

A barely visible quiver crossed her face; her eyes snapped open, fixed mine as she clutched my hand tight. "Promise me something, Honey—make sure you'll always be secure."

Make sure you'll always be secure—my mother's Gregorian chant, for my mother seemed to mistrust that God would have mercy on me. He hadn't had mercy on her, although she rarely mentioned her past. My mother loved to talk—about the news, the neighbors, her in-laws—but she didn't tell stories like my father, who loved to reminisce about World War Two. All I had from my mother were details gathered piecemeal through the years. She'd been born the month after Black Tuesday and grown up in the Depression. Money had been scarce.

Still, somehow my pharmacist grandfather managed to hold onto his store. My grandmother worked the counter and kept the books to help. My mother and her sister Marie, five years older than she, spent their childhood at home alone.

When I first put these bits together, I pictured my mother at five, my aunt at ten. I imagined them at the rowhouse on Avenue U (*Aven'U*) that I knew so well. It's summer, their parents are working, and they frolic freely in the heat like Tom Sawyer and Huckleberry Finn. They play hopscotch on the sidewalk beneath the shade of Trees of Heaven (the kind that do grow in Brooklyn) until they're tuckered out. Then they climb the steep front steps to the terrace that also serves as the landing to their house. There they rest at the iron table concealed from the street below by spreading Heavenly boughs and the terrace's hip-high stone wall. On the terrace, the air is cool, so they pass a few hours with Crayolas and Shirley Temple coloring books, intermittently pausing to admire their mother's potted blue hydrangeas and scarlet geraniums. When they tire from their art, they rise and go into the house, letting the screen door clap closed behind them. They head to the tiny back bedroom that overlooks the yard that even in that urban setting blooms sunflowers taller than a man. Lying on their shared bed, they doze to the lazy ticking of their father's desktop clock.

My grandparents' house wasn't much. The upstairs apartment they lived in had a small kitchen, a parlor and two bedrooms. It had a tiny pink bathroom with a skylight left open summer-long and never burgled by thieves (who waited seventy years to take my grandmother's Neapolitan cameo from my locked Seattle house). Downstairs was a second unit, which my grandparents rented out. It was the first place I lived.

Did my mother and aunt really grow up there? My mother never told me, and I never thought to ask. But when Mark and I became parents, I did ask for daycare advice. Still in her house on Long Island, my mother listened on the phone as I described the choices—institution, home daycare, au pair. She instantly made up her mind. I should choose an institution; there'd be lots of people around and supervision by the state. I should *never* leave my children in someone else's home or with a nanny in mine. I could never trust that "the woman" wouldn't leave Sean and Cristin alone while she went out to gallivant. That would terrify my kids. She said she knew this from experience. She'd spent her childhood waiting for a mother who'd abandoned her and her sister, left them locked in the house, where she'd been lonely and scared.

Josephine and Marie, named after the parents of Jesus. But their sacrifice wasn't a child, rather the presence of their mother. Daughters of the Depression left to raise themselves, no wonder my mother obsessed about savings and being alone. To her, money and a husband meant security.

As for money: My mother was the kind of person who'd drive ten miles out of her way to save a penny on a can of peas (which my sister, father and I hated). Before deciding where to shop, she'd scour the Sunday paper to find the best price around, and after she'd made her purchase, she'd triple check the ads to confirm she really had. For my mother there was nothing like a deal. I can still see her on the Europe trip our family took when I was twelve. We'd taken a ferry from Gibraltar to spend a few days in Tangier. On the day we'd planned to sail back, we were waiting for the ferry at the dock when a Moroccan man approached in a kaftan and fez. He was pushing a cart piled with blankets. Stopping right before us, he selected two nubby wool ones, each with a geometric pattern, one mostly orange, the other brown. He gestured to my mother: Want to buy a blanket for each of your girls?

My mother's eyes ignited. First she fingered the blankets, examined the weft and the warp. Then she held up her hand, slowly rubbing together her thumb and index finger. "How much?"

The man stretched up ten fingers, said something in Arabic.

My mother shook her head dramatically, countered with one finger.

He: eight.

She: two.

He: six.

She: two.

The ferry arrived. My mother shrugged her shoulders at the man, turned to my father, "Let's board the boat."

We climbed onto the gangplank, and as we stepped onto the deck, my mother looked over her shoulder, waved goodbye to the man.

He shouted something, snapped up two fingers.

My mother smiled. Nodding, she pulled out her wallet, rummaged round a bit, placed two coins on her palm, extending it over the gunwale so the man could see what it held. Then, he grunted, lobbed the blankets to my mother, and my mother tossed him the coins.

Not only did my mother bargain. While other mothers hired maids, mine dusted and vacuumed, scrubbed the toilet and tub, climbed on the eaves to ammonia the windows. While other mothers bought their daughter's dresses at Abraham and Strauss, mine took remnants from my father's father, stitched them into frocks on a second-hand Singer. While other mothers spent their days playing canasta, mine went to Harbor Elementary School and taught twenty-five kids. And each night when my father left the dinner table lighting up his cigar, she shook her head and muttered, "Burning a five-dollar bill."

But my mother never said this to my father. She never asked him to stop smoking in the car even though her eyes, my sister's and mine burned and teared as he drove. She never asked him to iron his own shirts—as a tailor's son, he knew how. She never asked him to go down to the basement to pull his boxers from the dryer himself. She didn't say *no* when my father retired and asked to move into her house, although he was left to clean the bathroom by himself.

I never asked her why she treated my father as she had. I never even wondered. Sister Agnes had early taught us *wives should be subordinate to their husbands as to the Lord.* Didn't nuns serve the priests' dinner? Didn't my mother serve my father's supper and my grandmothers my granddads'? Mr. Kohler even once explained that the Elizabethans viewed creation as a hierarchy: God, angels, men, women, animals, plants, rocks (why didn't it impress me then that rocks were at the bottom?). So it came as no surprise when I called my mother for counsel after Mark's and my first major fight. We'd been married for a year. He would soon graduate from law school and wanted to move back to New York. I was desperate to stay in Chapel Hill; it was sunny and far from my father. What was my mother's response? "It's the woman's job to bend." No, I never questioned this perspective until my mother was dead.

After my mother's death, I dreamed about the grotto—Mark and me walking hand-in-hand down a shady cypress-spired lane. It leads us to a garden—lemon trees, palms, white oleander, the air fragrant and warm. We follow a narrow path to a lawn—anemones ruffling in breeze, peacocks fanning turquoise tails. In the center is the grotto, celestial mother-of-pearl. Pristine, it's shaded by a graceful mulberry dripping red fruit.

"Jan, are you awake?"

Hearing Mark's voice, I started, saw the sign—Castelvetrano—fleet by the car.

"There's our exit. What do we do next? I tabbed the hospital in the guide."

I flipped through one of the travel guides that rested on my lap. "Here, it says:

Castelvetrano seems to have been a Greek town, though it was refounded by the Romans, who settled a colony of retired soldiers on it and gave it its present name—the castrum of the veterans. Salvatore Giuliano, the famous bandit, black marketer and separatist, was gunned down in Castelvetrano on July 5, 1950. The macabre scene of Giuliano's mother on her knees licking his blood off the pavement burns in the memory of many Sicilians. Later analysis proved that the blood belonged to a chicken."

"No, not the *Cadogan*—the *Michelin*."

I opened the slim green guide to a tabbed page:

"Castelvetrano is a small farming town primarily concerned with woodworking and the cultivation of vines and olive trees. The first impression of the town is tainted by the large glass building, the new hospital."

Mark motioned with his chin. "That must be it, right there." Merging onto the exit ramp, he decelerated the car, a gust of pink dust wafting from the road. It settled on the hood, revealing a jet-glass monolith.

"That can't be it," I said. "It's too new."

"We can go in and ask about the old one."

Like a star-gazing magus, Mark headed toward the tower. He turned onto a street lined by crumbling stucco shops trumpeting sidewalk wares—here a *fruttivendolo* with basketed eggplants, peppers, peaches, there a *pescheria* with ice-crated swordfish, clams, octopi. Gray-haired women watered geraniums on balconies strung with bras and boxers, some leaning over the railing to watch the scene below—Vespa-ed teens buzzing by Fiats, benched old men puffing cigars, shopkeepers peeking through door beads, thick-calved matrons hauling grocery bags.

We turned into a parking lot, our car reflecting in the windows of the new hospital. The lot bordered a stretch of lifeless, flaxen grass clumped in parched earth. Beyond it stood—or, rather, sank—a sprawling stone ruin. Low, shuttered with boards, Paradise trees spindling its roof, the building must have been abandoned decades before.

I climbed out of the car into the blistering heat, my family likewise. "Could that be it?"

We began to walk around the ruin, gray-green lizards darting into fissures as our feet crackled the grass and cicadas droned. Sean kicked a dead snake. Cristin coiled her hair, clipped it to the top of her head. Sweat trickled down my spine and between my breasts.

Mark turned a corner and we followed—another face of the building, this one heavily portaled by a shackled wooden door. Mark paused. "There you go."

Above the door was a broad stone lintel carved *Ospedale*. I turned to scan the area behind me. About sixty feet away was a scrubby knoll.

We walked silent, filed around it, skirting a rusty railing collapsed at its feet. The grotto—ivy shrouded, suckers crumbling its surface, shoot tips tasseling its mouth. Inside, bird-soiled Mary prayed with fingerless rosary-strung hands, and the altar, sooty, fractured, was ankle-deep in trash. Outside, in the porcelain photo, my grandmother, half my age, smiled above the tarnished plaque:

DONO DEL DOTTORE

PAOLO ERRANTE PARRINO

IN MEMORIA DELLA CONSORTE

Celeste Errante

Cristin took my hand, as I had taken my mother's the last time I saw her. With the toe of her sneaker, she ground a broken beer bottle neck into the thirsting sand. "I'm so sorry, Mommy."

I was sorry too. How much of what we think we know is fact, and how much fiction? How much of the history, the legends? How many of the places, the people? And how much of the love? Plato had imagined us cave prisoners who watch shadows cast by fire on the wall and confound them with reality. Why do we do that? My guess is that if we didn't, we couldn't watch at all.

Had Paulo really loved Celeste? The grotto intimates he did. But one year after he built it, he married Mimma there. And had Celeste really felt loved? Maybe Paolo demanded she work the pharmacy wholly against her will. Had Peter in fact loved Josephine? His leaving suggests he didn't. But he showed up for every family occasion—Christmas, birthdays, graduations—supported her all throughout her life; she never had to touch the nest egg she had saved. Had Josephine truly loved Peter? Maybe she married him for his law degree. And when he died and was cremated, she never reclaimed his ashes, never provided for their disposal. No grotto for my father; no stone for the Rock.

I looked at Mark. Did he love me? When I met him our Bucknell senior year, he was newly returned from Durham, England, where he'd spent nine months studying abroad. Rod Steward haircut, blue Shetland and jeans, he sat in the seat beside me on the first day of Art in the Dark , a.k.a. Art History 102. Lights out in auditorium, professor eulogizing Giotto, frescoes carouseled from a projector and paraded across a screen—*Meeting at the Golden Gate, Noli Me Tangere, The Virgin Receiving the Message, The Epiphany.* I jotted dates, titles, chapels, scribbled notes on style:

Strong undulat rhythms created by bldgs & landscape lead eye across scenes

Skies—deep blue foil for figures & sets—push them forward so they stand out

Subject—religious drama taking place in 3-D real world

Understatement & simplicity heighten emotion

Where other artists' figs gesticulate & grimace, Giotto's simply turn wrist, shift glance

Which is exactly what Mark did towards me: "Want a Lifesaver?" His hand was poised above my notebook, foiled five-flavor roll torn down to green.

I looked up from my page—his eyes, Giotto blue. "No thanks. I only like red."

He pried lime and orange off the roll, held the cherry out to me.

We became art history study partners, friends. I told him I'd transferred to Bucknell to escape my ex-boyfriend and parents. He showed me his England scrap book, the rubber-cemented mementoes precisely placed and neatly labeled: A photo: *Durham Cathedral and Castle*, "*Half Church of God, Half Castle 'gainst the Scot.*" (*Sir Walter Scott, 1817*). A bottle label: *New Castle Golden Jubilee Brown Ale—1927-1977.* A pound note, etched with Queen Elizabeth's portrait: *One Quid.* An invitation: *The Junior Common Room of St. Aiden's College Request the Pleasure of Your Company on the Occasion of Their Formal Dance.* A photo: *Isobel & The Debut of My New Suit.* Another photo: *Isobel among Crocuses at St. Aiden's College.* Still another: *Isobel Contemplating another Bite of Ice Cream at Hatfield College.* And yet one more: *Isobel in her Room at St. Aiden's College—The Identity of the Guy in the Picture* (not Mark) *Shall Rest in Obscurity Forever.*

And he meant it. Isobel, berry-lipped, Scottish, would always belong to Mark; he would see to that. Each week after art, we retrieved our college mail and he posted a letter to Isobel and received one back. And in June, just after college graduation, Isobel would journey to the States or Mark would travel to Scotland.

I imagined them as they had been together, he lying morning till evening beneath a sycamore in the Yorkshire moors, bees humming, heather purpling, bright white clouds flitting above. She, rocking in the rustling tree, among larks, throstles and cuckoos making music with the west wind, great swells of grasses undulating, as he recited Robert Burns:

As fair art thou, my bonnie lass,
So deep in luve am I;
And I will luve thee still, my dear,
Till a' the seas gang dry.
Till a' the seas gang dry, my dear,
And the rocks melt wi' the sun;

And I will luve thee still my dear,

While the sands o' life shall run.

Why hadn't Dave felt that for me, or my father for my mother? Oh, to be Isobel!

The night before our art midterm, Mark came to my room for a study session. He dropped his backpack on the rug, and we sat on the floor next to it. He pulled out his *Art Through the Ages*, his notebook and *Masterpiece Flashcards*.

I set the card box between us, took off the lid. "Okay, you draw."

Mark pulled a card from the box, held it before me: Adam waking from a nap, God presenting new-made Eve to him.

I smiled. "*The Garden of Earthly Delight*, Bosch, Flemish, Late Gothic." I slid the card from Mark's fingers, placed it on the rug, pulled another from the box: a golden-cloaked couple kneeling and embracing on a flowered crest.

Mark raised a dark-blond eyebrow. "*Der Kuss*, Klimt, Austrian Symbolist." I plunked the card on the pile; he plucked the next: a dark-suited man rowing a woman and bonneted baby on a lake.

I nodded. "*The Boating Party*, Mary Cassatt, American Impressionist."

Mark placed the card in the stack. "You know, I'm kind of hungry. Would you like a little snack?"

"Sure, but we'll have to go out. There's no food in the room."

"That's okay. I brought some." He opened up his backpack, extracted Saltines, Easy Cheese, Mateus, a corkscrew, two paper plates and cups. He spritzed spirals of cheese on some crackers, arranged them in circles on a plate. He pulled the cork from the bottle, poured wine to the brims of the cups. He winked, raised his cup to clink.

An hour later, we were laughing—*juiced on Mateus, just hanging loose*. A half-hour more and he kissed me. Then he turned out the lights, and we studied art in the dark.

Waking up the next morning, Mark apologized. He hadn't acted from the right motives; he'd received a letter from Isobel: she'd found another guy, a Brit with a guitar. But Mark was still in love with her.

I cried. What did Isobel have that I didn't have that earned Mark's devotion? But I knew: raven hair, violet eyes, a brogue and Anglo-Saxon pedigree. But she didn't love him; I did.

Mark stuffed his things in his backpack, turned to walk out my door. "Good luck on the exam. Sorry to drag you in."

But it happened again a few weeks later—the wine, the romance, the contrition. My tears, his walking out. The next time, though, there was no penitence, no mention of the Scottish lass.

Two years later, we were still together. We'd set up house in a Chapel Hill apartment—my Sicilian pottery as knickknacks, his British beer mat collection on the walls. In the morning, he perked the Folgers. In the evening, I simmered pasta sauce. We put up a tiny tree on Christmas, trimmed it with ornaments from Woolworth. We packed a picnic supper Independence Day, oohed and ahhed at the fireworks show. We'd married our records together—my Elton John, his Little Feat, our double Beatles. But never once had Mark even hinted he'd ever marry me.

At first, the question sporadically whispered in my mind, but with time came to incessantly shout: Why live in sin, dink around in Dixie, slaughter rats in a research lab, if I wasn't in Mark's plans?

One October afternoon, it exploded. We were crossing Franklin Street from the U.N.C. quad the day I learned Holly Brown was engaged. She'd been twinkling her diamond at the lab crew: "Suga', how 'bout a hug for good luck?"

I said it in the middle of the street, the idea birthed on the spot. "Mark, just to let you know, since you apparently have no intention of marrying me, I've decided to join the Peace Corps."

He pulled me onto the sidewalk, huddled me against a store. "You what?"

"Decided to sign up for the Peace Corps! Just admit it. I've always been your rebound, your Isobel default!"

He pushed my hair behind my ears, eyes scouring my face. "You want to get married?"

I started to cry.

"Jesus, Jan. Okay."

That day, I called my parents with the news: the wedding date would be in May. But Mark didn't call his:

October 14: "Mark, did you tell your parents?"

"No, Jan. Not yet."

October 21: "Mark, did you tell your parents?"

"Not yet, Jan. I have a test."

October 28: "Mark, did you tell your parents?"

"No. I'll tell them soon."

November 4: I handed him the Princess phone. "Damn it, Mark, call now."

Mark dialed the number. I heard his mother's "Hello" down the line. Mark delivered the message. I heard his mother's pause. Mark waited on the line. I heard his mother's "But she's Italian!"

Had that been the hindrance all along? Jan, the female Fonz? Jan, the Papist Wop?

Still, there we were in Sicily, nineteen years into our marriage. He'd planned the trip to ease my mourning for my mother, done it on his own, as a surprise. He'd tabbed the pages of the guidebooks so I'd see every church, garden, ancient ruin. He'd reserved lovely *pensioni*, each with a view of the sea. But would I one night be in our kitchen, setting our pasta to boil, and receive a call from Cristin that he'd found a lover, wasn't coming home? And would I ever leave Mark? Did we love each other like a rock?

I kneeled at the foot of the grotto's altar, eyes skimming the garbage lying there. I picked up a brittle plastic bag, turning to my clan. "Let's clean it before we go."

Cristin squatted beside me. We scooped refuse in the bag— Sammontana ice cream wrappers, crushed Orange Fanta cans, dirt, decomposing leaves, a grubby Camel package, a wooden rosary with no cross. Mark found some Bounty in his backpack, wiped my grandmother with his spit. Sean picked up scattered pages of a faded *Gazzetta dello Sport.*

After, we walked back to the car, tossing the garbage in a dumpster. As the kids slid into their seats, Mark opened the trunk and stashed his backpack. I noticed the tool kit in the trunk well, which I'd not seen before. It seemed to call to me.

I reached for the kit, untied the knot. I unrolled it, pulled a Phillips out. "Let's go back—I have an idea."

"What?"

"Just come. You'll see."

At the grotto, I fitted the Phillips into a copper plaque screw, twisted, but no luck. Understanding, Mark took it from my grip, torqued the first screw, the second, third and fourth. On the grotto's surface, four holes and a clean pink rectangle. Mark slipped the screws in his pocket, handed me the tarnished plaque.

Taking Heart

I tightened the laces of my sneakers, pressed the headphones of my iPod snugly over my ears and began to walk the Green Lake path. Striding to the rhythm of "Belle Speranze," I tried to focus on the positive aspects of the day. Sunbeams streaming through high drifting clouds, light breeze gusting cool and fresh. Weeping willows fronds brushing the lake, yellow irises bobbing on the banks. I perused the other people at the park. Joggers whizzing by, hair streaming back, pairs of chatting mothers pushing strollers. Dog walkers pausing to let pets sniff the grass, everybody smiling. I breathed in deeply, pumped my arms and legs. Maybe some exertion would help dull the blade of my grief.

Certainly on that summer day there was plenty of news that might have troubled me. I could have been thinking about the parents of soldiers lately massacred in Iraq. I could have been praying for the mothers and fathers of students recently slaughtered at Virginia Tech. But that morning the losses of others didn't even prick the epidermis of my consciousness. For I too had lost much-loved children; I'd lost my job at Moshe Ben Maimon.

Just a few days before, I'd spent a Saturday grading final papers. The assignment had required the juniors to write responses to five of nine literature prompts. There was no single right answer to any of the questions, should have been as many interpretations as students in the class. It was a sound assignment pedagogically, designed to stimulate high-order thinking, empower kids with choice. A smart assignment pragmatically, planned to discourage student cheating, mitigate teacher boredom (mine). Nearing the bottom of the pile, I placed Dinah's paper on the desk:

In seventeenth century Massachusetts, religion dictates behavior. In *The Scarlet Letter,* the city of Boston is ruled by two entities, the Governor and the Church. Though Governor Bellingham is the representative of the city, he governs with the Church at his side.

Dictated, entities, governed? Dinah's vocabulary was improving! I underlined the three words, jotted in the margin: *Good, clear opening. Great word choice!,* read on:

Hester Prynne's punishment for committing adultery is to stand on the scaffold in the center of town with a scarlet letter "A" pinned to her chest, and to live out the rest of her life in a state of seclusion, always wearing the eminent scarlet letter.

I circled *eminent,* wrote *prominent?,* paused: Have I seen this error before?

While Hester stands on the scaffold, the Governor directs an inquisition as to with whom she had sinned, directing the young reverend Arthur Dimsdell to plead with Hester, telling him that he is responsible to protect her soul. The cooperation between the Governor and Reverend Dimsdell shows the strong link between the Church and the government of the United States.

I underlined *as to with whom,* wrote *awkward phrasing,* circled *Dimsdell,* jotted *misspelled,* underlined *the United States,* scribbled *In the 1600s?* A trifecta of mistakes I then recognized. I yanked Galia's paper from the stack, skimmed it and Dinah's side by side.

Damn. Another plagiarism.

How I hated plagiarism. Time wasted cross-checking, writing memoranda, meeting principals, students, parents. Gut-wrenching denials, admissions, betrayals. Painful excuses, sanctions, tears. I heaved a sigh, retrieved the essay pile, reexamined it line by line, discovered:

1. Four students had chosen the same five questions. No other students had done so.

2. Ezra and Nurit's work was identical, down to font, spacing and typos (signs of beginning cheating).
3. Dinah's paper matched Ezra's and Nurit's, except for font and some substituted synonyms (traits of intermediate).
4. Galia's paper corresponded to Dinah's, except for font, corrected typos and a few additional sentences (sophisticated plagiarism).
5. All four had made the same mistakes of fact.

Jeez guys, why do you do this? To me, your parents, yourselves?

Normally when I detected plagiarism, I summoned the suspects after school, chided their *yarmulkes* and scrunchies as they became transfixed by the carpet, Rabbi's Schwartz's amoebic coffee stains (of which there were many). I spread the evidence before them, watched their lower lips tremble, listened to the silence rumble, pressure hiss, pleas and pretexts explode:

"I'm sorry! Please don't tell my parents!"

"I hate this school! There's too much homework!"

"But my father says I have to get into Penn!"

And I'd try to be compassionate and firm.

Maybe I was sometimes too merciful. I wasn't one of those teachers who screamed and applied rules rigidly; I tried to listen, take circumstances into account. I didn't run a classroom dictatorship; I sought a democratic path. I wasn't one of those teachers who berated; I strove to practice reason and kindness, model the world I wished to live in.

And generally it worked. Many of my students claimed to love the supportive nature of our class, said it helped them learn (a compliment I thrived on). Most of my students were honest. But there were always a few who took advantage.

Like Galia. In truth, I loathed that girl. Her continual chatter during classes, even after pointed castigation (flutter of long lashes,

"Chava and I were just talking about the *literature*!"). Frequent failure to turn in assignments, saccharine pleas for extensions (cough, cough, "But I've been so *ill*!"). Constant conniving for extra points, even on incomplete papers (flick of blond mane, "But I worked so *hard*!") Repeated accusations that I'd mislaid her work, delays in providing replacements (pout of L'Oreal lips, "But I turned it *in*!").

I had no doubt her final was a fraud, that she and her friends had cheated. Classes were over, no time to waste; I emailed the kids. And I copied their parents and Charles Freund, Moshe Ben Maimon's secular studies dean:

Hi All—

I noticed that the four of you turned in almost identical final literature responses. Several of you even had the same typos. You know our class contract provides that both the giver and recipient of responses receive 0s for copied assignments. Consequently, I can't give you credit for your finals. I will also be reporting the incident to Mr. Freund, who may decide to enforce the school's cheating policy. Cheating is not acceptable. Colleges expel students for it. As juniors, you need to learn this. I'm sorry this happened.

I tapped send. It was out of my hands. Charles would handle it on Monday.

Later, in the evening, I told Mark about the incident. We were strolling to Salvatore, our favorite restaurant. We passed a neighbor's street-side garden—yellow pear tomatoes rambling trellises, rows of red sail lettuces, citrus jasmine on a lattice fence. "What a nice night," I said. "How about Chianti with dinner?"

"Sure, what are we celebrating?"

"Well, I just finished grading. Can you believe, four juniors cheated, turned in the same final paper. I'm so glad to be done!"

How many times since that evening have those words echoed in my head: *I'm so glad to be done!* And I wonder: If I hadn't said them, would my lot have been the same?

What did I expect would happen? What normally happened with plagiarism. That four penitent confessions would be waiting in my Sunday morning in-box. That I'd reward earnest contrition, offer partial credit for honest make-up work. But admissions didn't greet me in the morning. Instead, from Dinah:

mrs. vallone—

i am unsure as to what you are referring to but i can assure you that i didnt cheat or copy. i will be more then glad to discuss this with you but i dont know where this is even coming from.

From Galia:

Hey:

I'm just having a difficult time understanding how my work can be "almost identical" to the other students' when the most I did was simply discuss. I completely formulated my own writing without the help or work of any other student. I used my own words and I phrased things myself. In no way did I copy or even see the work of another student.

From Nurit:

Dear Ms. Vallone,

i understand your concern, but i can honestly PROMISE you that we didnt cheat—or at least i didnt i cant know for sure about the others. yes we did talk about the answers, but we didnt send each other anyhting. i had some questions about them and i am sure i just asked galia what she wrote so i could write something along the lines of it.

also, what errros are you talking about? because it is impossible for all of us to have the same errors when we did not cheat! i seriously dont know what to do to prove this to you. i really did not cheat!

A match-flick to a stack of kindling. What, do they think I'm stupid? In previous cheating situations, kids claimed they'd emailed work to classmates meaning only to lend them ideas, or had brainstormed questions with buddies or based responses on comments made in class. But while I certainly understood that teens find it hard saying *no* to desperate friends and was flattered to imagine students discussed or even thought about my class, I'd made it clear *ad nauseam* that they were to write independently. Thus the question arose: What were the odds that a foursome working on their own would select the same quintet of questions, craft the same paragraphs and sentences, choose and misuse the same words?

And what, pray tell, about those typos?

Come on, guys, get real!

Still, I genuinely wanted to give them the benefit of the doubt, so I re-scrutinized all of the papers, presented the evidence to my home court:

Said Mark: "They obviously cheated."

Said Cristin: "Pshh, yeah!"

Her friend Ben: "You're kidding; they thought you wouldn't notice?"

Said Sean: "Mom, just give them Fs!"

Thus, I rested my case.

Monday I woke up confident—sunlight on my pillow, my cat paw-pumping my back, a woodpecker in the horse chestnut, dhakdhakdhak dhakdhakdhak. I rose and read my email. From Galia's father (a professor), copy to Dean Freund and Rabbi Schwartz:

Mrs. Vallone:

Galia did not cheat. I can only attribute similarities between her responses and those of the others as reflecting the intensity of their study together; they pooled their collective understanding of the different texts (misconceptions and all), studied together diligently (Galia often studies to the point of memorization), and regurgitated the same literature responses.

From Ezra's father (a psychiatrist):

Dear Ms. Vallone,

It appears that you're assuming a conspiracy. Maybe a group email is not such a great idea for making this accusation. I don't want to know about the humiliation of other children and their families. If they want to tell me, that is their business. It is embarrassing to many people, and the harm is greater than the benefit. It is just like being put in the stocks in the city square with an accusation hung around your neck. By the way, that is why I have not made my response public but am writing my criticism directly to you and to you only.

As I read, a corkscrew coiled through my viscera, was wrenched from my bowels to my head. Studied diligently together? Can't you see they're recidivist cheaters! Stocks in the city square? Don't you know what your kids put me through?

Suddenly I saw my students reflected in a funhouse mirror—large, looming, jeering. Boaz who refused to remove his earphones while I was trying to teach a class, then wrestled for his iPod when I tried to remove it from his desk. Dov, who retrieved the gum I'd confiscated, took it from my purse when I turned my back, then blew a huge pink bubble, popped it in front of my face. Tzivya, who answered her cell phone in the middle of a test, snipped, "Just *wait* a *min*ute" when I asked her to hang up. Kelila, who said *sotto voce* while we were discussing Romeo and Juliet, "I know exactly what happened! He made her pussy wet!"

Then there was Ovid (Galia's older brother). Daily between classes he sneaked into my classroom leaving magic marker drawings on the whiteboard: a crucified green Jesus, Jewish star on a chain around his neck, fuchsia blood oozing from nail holes, orange text ballooning from his mouth: *See you later, Gator!*

All of which I'd handled with composure, reason, tact.

Stocks in the city square? I'm the nicest teacher at the school!

• • • • •

Charles Freund summoned me to school that Monday afternoon. Pudgy, sweater-vested, white haired, with blue bespectacled eyes, Charles was selfless, kind, soft-spoken, loyal, humble, generous, wise. Charles was a real-world Mr. Rogers, an overstuffed fireside chair. And, oh, I loved him like a father. He'd given me my chance to be a teacher, frequently praised and thanked me, treated me like a star. Once he'd even written:

Jan, early in her career, is on her way to teaching greatness. God, said a famous architect, is in the details. Jan has worked out, in elaborate detail, the learning her students will do. The Moshe Ben Maimon School is extraordinarily fortunate that Jan left the legal profession, became a teacher and found her way to us.

His words, to me Dom Pérignon. They made me dream that one day I'd be honored, like the best teachers at the school, with a lavish dinner at the Olympic Hotel and a Tehillah Teaching Award (parents and students applauding). They made me believe God *was* in the details, that teaching was my calling—God's gift for my old age, earned by hard work and sacrifice. They made me dogged to do anything for Charles—my benefactor, mentor, friend—especially since he suffered from Parkinson's, his tremors quaking my heart.

When I arrived at his office, Charles asked me to sit at his table, put his cane aside, took a seat himself. So many pleasant hours we'd passed there during my six years at Moshe Ben Maimon. Often after school on Fridays we'd talked kids, curriculum and education among his piled-high stacks—attendance forms, P.S.A.T. pamphlets—surrounded by shelves of books—*Warriner's*, *Great Expectations*. But that day Charles said nothing, studied his hands clasped upon the table, rubbing thick thumbs around.

He cleared his throat, eyes still averted. "Jan, you need to apologize to the parents and kids."

Normally I'm a whiz at the art of self–blame and remorse. Lightly tap my guilt button, and my tongue propels apologies like an arcade machine flips pin balls. But that time, for some reason, my penitence lever was jammed. "Apologize? What for?"

Charles looked up at me. "You publicly humiliated the families. Sending a group email was insensitive and misguided."

In my chest, pecking like a hatching chick. I hadn't hesitated a moment to send a collective email, never doubted my principles and prudence. In any legal action, the law requires plaintiffs to jointly name and notify all parties, including the parents of minors. "Charles, I don't see that. I meant to be open and fair. Surely the parents know their children's friends. And the kids—they cheated *together*."

His hands began to shake. "Jan, for goodness sake! You need to apologize!"

And then I detected it: fear. That's what I heard in his voice. Were the parents threatening to withhold donations from the school? Or bring a libel lawsuit? But libel requires malice; clearly, there was none of that. I measured my voice. "Charles, I did nothing wrong. I'd rather resign than retract."

At that, the seismic waves amplified, radiated from his hands. Up his arms to his neck. To his chin to his nostrils and eyebrows. He snatched a tissue from a box, blotted his forehead, but the tremors intensified.

He slammed the table with his hand. I lurched back in my seat. Pencils rolling to the floor. "Damn it, Jan!"

Behind by ribs, thrashing wings. I gaped, bit my tongue.

His mouth contorted, trickled spit. He dabbed it with the tissue. "You'd think with all those years of law, you'd know about privacy rights!"

The cleaving of my chest. Who did he think he was? "Charles, get this straight! You can say anything you want about my teaching, but

I'm the only one sitting here who knows *anything at all* about the law!"

Narrowing eyes, he aimed his arrow. "That's it! I accept your resignation!"

Suddenly all was quiet. I tried to steady my breath, realized I was sobbing. I felt his stare, heard the ticking of a clock. I stood, "Thank you, Charles." I walked out of the room.

Later that day, I emailed the parents, individually this time:

Dear Mr. and Mrs. X,

I would like to assure you that I meant absolutely no harm by sending my email relating to the literature responses I received from several of the juniors in my class. I sent it without any intent whatsoever to ridicule or shame any student or parent. I sent it after spending several hours cross-checking responses against each other and drawing conclusions based upon my experience as a teacher. I believed it best to contact all four students together, since they would naturally want to know whose responses were implicating theirs. I also believed it best to contact their parents simultaneously because I regard this type of student conduct to be very serious. It hurts the students who do it by interfering with true learning and exposing them to painful sanctions that will only become more painful the higher in the educational system they climb.

I am truly sorry for any displeasure or discomfort my email may have caused. That was the very opposite of my intent. I care enormously about my students and try to serve them and their families the very best that I can at all times.

Such a lawyerly letter. I read it now with pride, self-righteousness, sorrow, embarrassment, pain. I didn't know at the time I wrote it that I'd receive no response, my words melting in the sun, lost in summer break's bustle as my colleagues dispersed to Spain and France, my students to six-week Jewish camps, their parents to Jerusalem. I didn't know I'd never know how Moshe Ben Maimon resolved the episode or what, if anything at all, my students and colleagues were told of my departure. I didn't know that come fall Charles would replace me with a bearded teacher half my age, that no high school would hire me again, that I'd be left wondering: Had I been tactless and foolish? Had Charles meant the good things he'd once said? Had I done to my students what Mrs. Dixon had done to Sean? How could I say those things to Charles? How could I make him shake? Was teaching really my calling, or had I imagined it?

As I rounded a bend at Green Lake, my iPod shuffled to a more *andante* tune—*I see you Mary in the garden / In the garden of a thousand sighs / There's holy pictures of our children / Dancin' in a sky filled with light.* I quickened my pace to match the beat, pumped my limbs harder. Over and over, images flickered in my mind: Galia's equine teeth, pencils on the floor. Ezra in the stocks, a goblet of red wine. My classroom's empty seats, Jesus on the cross.

Jesus. I remember first hearing his story from my cousin Angela one Easter Sunday. I was probably five and Angela eight, and we were sitting on the front steps of her family's house in Levittown, each of us in a gathered spring dress with a bow tied at the back. Easter baskets resting on our laps, mine yellow, Angela's pink, she spoke as she pealed the foil from a chocolate Easter egg. She told me Jesus was the son of God and that he never sinned. God had given him special powers so he could do miracles. Once he fed a big crowd with just one fish and a loaf of bread. He healed the sick, made the blind see and even brought dead people back to life. But there were some rulers who thought it wrong for Jesus to do those things, so they arrested him. They stripped him almost naked, whipped him and gave him a crown of thorns. They nailed him on a cross, hammering spikes through his hands and feet. They raised the cross on a mountain and Jesus hung to death, sun burning his skin, body dripping lots of blood. Then he was buried and rose.

When she finished the story, Angela popped the egg in her mouth and started de-foiling another. My stomach roiled as I watched. "Why did God let Jesus die?"

She smiled, gums and teeth stained chocolate. "It was part of God's plan."

Forty years later, I would tell my students our goal as readers was to strive to learn from stories, especially passion-filled stories like Elie Wiesel's, Huckleberry Finn's, Romeo and Juliet's, Hester Prynne's. We had to walk in the characters' shoes, try to discern how the world functioned and use the knowledge we gained to improve it and ourselves. But I never understood the Jesus story, not the first time I heard it, nor the many times since, nor when I recalled it while walking at Green Lake. Was I supposed to observe that giving our best earns nothing but contempt, rejection rather than love? Was I supposed to conclude that to some our best is bad? Is *good* just the perspective of the moment's majority? Or is there a universal *good* that we should do for better or worse? And was I supposed to trust that injured do-gooders would one day rise up? Or accept that having done *good* would be the only reward? Had people invented Heaven because *good* doesn't pay in this life?

See you later, Gator! That's what Ovid's Jesus said. But I didn't want to accept that; I wanted Charles and my students back.

Truly, I loved my students. I delighted in their sagacity, silliness, affection. I relished their *chutzpah*, ebullience, took pride in their growth. Like Zach, curly-haired, gray-eyed, who stopped doing his homework when his brother died of cancer, barely passed my junior class. Then, as a senior he gave a speech to teens whose loved-ones were ill:

When my brother passed away, I thought I would never get past it. Then I worked on a story about him with a teacher who saw some potential in me. A few months later, I learned that my story had placed second in a contest. It is going to be published and distributed worldwide. If just one person reads my story and is consoled or gains an insight from it, I will have done what I thought impossible—brought hope and optimism out of sadness.

Or Akiva, with his brown-eyes and baseball motif *yarmulke*, who whined in freshman English, "We have to write short stories? What a waste of time!" Then, as a junior he founded and edited a journal:

Last month, I was wandering the halls thinking, *There has to be a way for people in the Moshe Ben Maimon community to express themselves.* I came up with the idea of a literary journal that would provide students, faculty and staff with a place to write and read the beautiful writing of others. Through several lunchtime meetings with Mr. Freund and Ms. Vallone, I was able to initiate *Kol Rinah.* Just think, once I was excited at the *idea* of having a literary journal, and now I'm almost dancing with elation at the *reality.* I am exceptionally pleased to present to you the first issue of *Kol Rinah.*

Or Shoshana, with her blue-eyes, rainbow-striped leggings and polka-dotted boots, who claimed *Night* was giving her nightmares about her *sabbah* at Treblinka. She refused to finish the book. Then, later that semester, she wrote a reflective paper:

Ms. Vallone told me she would not force me to finish, but sometimes there are challenges in life that cause you pain. It is necessary to learn to deal with the pain, and sometimes the pain can be inspirational. She gently explained that I needed to try to find the beauty in the book. So, I finished it. Every chapter was a struggle. But it describes many beautiful acts of kindness that people did in the midst of so much evil. Thinking of the beauty helped me deal with the pain, like when Eliezer

gave his soup to his dying father even though Eliezer needed it
to survive. This gave me the strength I was lacking.

Zach, Akiva, Shoshona. Darren, Yasmin, Michal. Ariel, Uri, Miri.
I'd agonized about them in the wake of the recent shooting, the worst
in Seattle history. Late one afternoon, a man had entered the building
of the Jewish Federation armed with two semi-automatic pistols.
Tramping up a hallway, he yelled, "I'm angry with Israel," sprayed
bullets into offices, wounded three women in the gut, killed a fourth by
gunning her head. As he squeezed the trigger at a fifth, she embraced
her pregnant belly, saved herself and her unborn child. I'd prayed to be
as quick as she had been if this were to happen at our school, prayed to
protect my students as I'd protect Cristin and Sean. How would I ever
live without my students if they died? How would ever live without
them now that I'd lost my job?

As I marched around the lake, I wished I could talk to my mother.
She had moved to Seattle when my father died, when her breast cancer
was first diagnosed. We'd often walked around Green Lake engrossed in
conversation. What would she say if she knew that I'd given up law for
teaching? What would she say if I told her I'd found myself by finding
her in me, found myself by helping youngsters find themselves? What
would she say if she knew I'd found something I loved and somehow
lost it? What would she say if I asked her if I'd ever teach again? I knew
exactly what she'd say: One step at a time. She said it when her cancer
was confined and she could walk Green Lake unassisted. She said it
when the cancer reached her bones and she wobbled the path on her
walker. She said it when the cancer reached her liver and I pushed her
wheelchair around the lake.

So I walked. And as I did, something floated into view—a red blur
coursing on the breeze. Above my head, it collided with the branches

of a weeping willow by the path. Peering up the tree trunk, I spotted a dangling tangled ribbon, reached up and tugged it. The object dislodged from its niche, and as I pulled, it scraped down the branches as through rungs on a wooden ladder. I drew the object to my chest—a heart-shaped helium balloon, its crimson surface scratched, bruised like a cracking scab, revealing the smooth tensile layer of healthy skin beneath. And it was still buoyant. So I tied the ribbon round my wrist and let the heart rise up, let it bob above my head as I walked on.

Epilogue

When I was a child, I used to talk as a child, think as a child, reason as a child; when I became a man, I put aside childish things.

At present we see indistinctly, as in a mirror, but then face to face. At present I know partially; then I shall know fully, as I am fully known.

So faith, hope, love remain, these three; but the greatest of these is love.

—*1 Corinthians 13: 11-13*

• • • • •

Ben Bag Bag would say: Delve and delve into it, for all is in it; see with it; grow old and worn in it; do not budge from it, for there is nothing better.

—*Pirkei Avot: 5.21*

Uncle Mario

I'm in room 224 at Port Saint Lucie Medical Center; that's my recording studio. It's about 1:30 a.m., and I have started to record at this hour because the nurses don't give you an opportunity to do a damn thing until they're ready. Frankly, I think they're all sadists. They've taken my pulse and whatever they want to take and given me my dinner and some shots. So far I've had my blood drawn four times and have one, two, three, four, five I.V. bags. They make certain you get no rest or freedom. However, I get by with my little machinations, like calling home and asking them to bring me some linguini with white clam sauce. To hell with the food downstairs.

Actually they do a good job here at Saint Lucie Medical Center.

But I'm not here to tell you about the hospital. I want tell you about my Uncle Mario, although he really wasn't my Uncle Mario; he was my cousin Pete from Uncle Willie's Uncle Mario. Uncle Willie was my father's older brother, and he was married to my Aunt Mary, who was Uncle Mario's sister. Out of respect, I called him Uncle Mario.

You noticed that when I referred to my cousin Pete, I indicated he was Pete from Uncle Willie. In my family, that designation was very necessary. My father's family was creative when it came to naming their children. Every first son was named after my grandfather Pietro, which means in my family there were four Peters. So when you talk about one of us, you have to identify: Peter from Uncle Mike, Peter from Uncle Charlie, Peter from Uncle Willie or Peter from Uncle Sam.

Actually, the Peter problem got worse when we were confirmed. You know that upon confirmation, a boy takes as his middle name the first name of his godfather. Now this custom would have been a very useful thing if we Peters had different godfathers. Except, my family had a little problem. Although our Uncle James didn't have children, he had all the money! So all of us chose him as godfather, whereafter we had Peter J. from Uncle Mike, Peter J. from Uncle Charlie, Peter J. from Uncle Willie and Peter J. from Uncle Sam.

Sam? He was my father. You may wonder how the hell in 1903 a good Italian boy gets named Sam. Well, it really didn't happen back that far. It was about 1916 when Pop was employed by an outfit in the City of New York. The name, as I recall, was Sidney J. Rohr, and they manufactured ladies' garments. At that time, Pop was a shipping clerk, and Mr. Rohr called him into the office one day. He sat him down and said, "Salvatore, we want to promote you to the head of the department. However, this is a Jewish organization, and we deal with a lot of Jewish people and they can't handle a name like Salvatore. So, we have to change your name. We can't call you Sol; we already have a Sol. So from here on, if you want the raise and the job, your name will have to be Sam. Is that okay?"

Pop said, "It's okay!" So thereafter, he was Sam.

As an aside, Sam married Esther, my mother, who had gone to a parochial school up in Harlem. When they first registered her there, they brought her in to the Mother Superior who questioned her about her name. Mom said, "Pasqua," which means *Easter* in Italian. That threw the Irish nun into a tizzy. She thought it sacrilegious to be named Easter, so she changed Mom's name, and thereafter called her Esther. So here we have a fine Italian family full of Jewish names.

Is all of this clear to you now? Then, let's get back to Uncle Mario.

I vividly recall Election Day, 1936, when I was about eleven. It was about 8 p.m., and at that time just about every corner in the City of New York was adorned by a bonfire celebrating the fact that people in this country could go out and elect their leaders freely. These fires were so enormous that their flames seemed to lick the facades of the buildings, or pretty close. Well, I was on East Twelfth Street in Manhattan, walking in an easterly direction toward a fire, when I noticed Uncle Mario coming in the opposite direction. He appeared to be stepping out from the bowels of hell, wearing his usual sharkskin suit, sharkskin coat, dapper fedora and big fat cigar. I say wearing the cigar because it was perfectly balanced in his mouth, and he just puffed it maybe every ten seconds, enough to emit a nice little ball of smoke. "Hello, Uncle Mario!" I said.

He responded in his usual gregarious, garrulous manner. "Hey Kid! Say hello to your father!"

I said, "Yes, Uncle Mario!" and walked on, but he called back, "Hey Kid! You good?"

"Yes, Uncle Mario!" I said.

He nodded. "You'd better be, 'cause if you're not, I'll kick you in the can!"

When I returned home I advised my father that Uncle Mario sent him greetings. Pop appeared kind of surprised. "He's back?"

So I asked him, "From where?"

"College," he said.

College? What the hell did I know about college? This was the Depression, and I lived in an immigrant neighborhood, where all they ever did was open fruit boxes. They'd sell a few apples so they'd get a few bucks. So I asked my father, "What's college?," and he told me it was a school where you lived on the premises and they teach you to do various things like carpentry, metal work, laundry, tailoring and license plates. At that point, I was intrigued. College sounded easy, and I figured it paid off on account of Uncle Mario's fancy sharkskin suits. So I decided one day I'd go to college.

Two or three years went by. Pop had lost his job, so he was making some money at home, manufacturing custom-tailored riding britches and tennis shorts for the rich and infamous, such as the Rockefellers, the Brewsters and the Astors. In 1939, he decided he may as well go into business. So he rented some space just east of Fifth Avenue on Seventeenth Street, with a room about twenty by thirty, and put in a couple of sewing machines, a couple of wooden horses with an old door across the top for a cutting table, a pressing board with an iron and a few other appliances he needed to make it a factory.

Well, after my father was there just about a week, some character comes through the door. He tells my father the premium for protection will be one hundred dollars per week to be picked up by one of his associates every Friday at 5 p.m. This really shook Pop up, so that night he tells Uncle Willie, and Uncle Willie tells Aunt Mary, and Aunt Mary tells Uncle Mario. Like a shot, Uncle Mario is up in our apartment and wants to know what's going on. So Pop tells him, and Uncle Mario advises Pop that he will see him Friday at the factory at 5 p.m.

Well, on that specific day and at that specific time, the character comes walking through the door of Pop's factory with his hand extended for the premium. Uncle Mario comes out of the back room. Wearing his sharkskin suit, his cigar dangling from his mouth, he places one hand under each of the man's armpits and drags him out backwards. Pop never sees the man again and no one asks for any more handouts.

Well, the years rolled on. World War Two came around with the bombing of Pearl Harbor. I spent four years in the service, and upon my return I went to college and law school. Then I started working on a law practice, married and had two daughters.

I didn't think much of Uncle Mario anymore. Eventually Aunt Mary died, and like a good nephew, I went to the wake. When I arrived, my cousin Pete from Uncle Willie escorted me up to the casket, where I said a few prayers and turned to leave with cousin Pete.

As we were moving out of the premises, I notice a very large sofa with a little man sitting in the middle, his elbows on his knees, his head cradled in his hands, and he is sobbing away. So I ask my cousin Pete, "Who's he?"

"Don't you remember Uncle Mario?

"Oh, yeah!"

"You know, he lost some of his eyesight, so he's retired now and they have him in an apartment up at Riverside Drive. He has a nice balcony up there overlooking the Hudson River, and on a nice day, he sits outside with his binoculars and watches the boats go up and down."

I looked back at Uncle Mario. He was more composed now, blowing smoke balls from his fat cigar. Then I remembered a newspaper article I'd read a while back. It was about a Mafioso, Don "The Cigar" Galante, who was about to be let out of jail. He was a notorious hit man, the toughest mobster in New York. No one could even estimate the number of murders he committed since he gave his victims cement shoes and dropped them into the Hudson.

And I say, "Hey, Pete, I always wondered, which college did he go to?"

"Uncle Mario? Sing-Sing. But we don't talk about that!"

Signing off,

Peter J. Raconteur

About the Author

Born in Brooklyn and raised on Long Island, Jan Vallone is the granddaughter of Sicilian immigrants. She practiced law for eighteen years in Manhattan and Seattle before becoming a high school English teacher and currently teaches writing at a Pacific Northwest university. When she is not writing or teaching, she enjoys reading, gardening, traveling and spending time with her husband, children and friends.

www.janvallone.com

Pieces of Someday
Reading Group Guide

READING GROUP QUESTIONS
AND DISCUSSION TOPICS

1. Visualize a scene in the memoir the setting of which is especially vivid in your memory. Describe the particular sights, objects, colors, sounds, smells and sensations that you associate with the scene and explain how the author made the setting come alive for you.

2. Recall a scene in the memoir the atmosphere of which is especially palpable in your memory. Describe the emotions that came over you as you were reading the scene and explain how the author aroused those emotions in you.

3. Imagine the narrator of the memoir and describe what she is like. Describe how you reacted to the narrator and explain how the author made her come alive for you.

4. Which person in the memoir would you most like to meet? Describe what he or she is like and explain why you would like to meet him or her.

5. Recall a major conflict that someone in the memoir faced. Describe what it was and how he or she handled it. Describe circumstances in which you have already or might in the future face a similar conflict and explain whether you did or would handle it as in the memoir.

6. Recall your impression of the narrator at the beginning of the memoir and your impression of her at the end. Describe how she changes as a result of her experiences.

7. State an insight about one of the following that a reader might derive from reading the memoir and explain why he or she might derive that insight. Describe circumstances in your own life in which you have come to the same or the opposite insight and explain why.

   a. truth/falseness

   b. beauty/ugliness

   c. morality/immorality

   d. power/weakness

   e. kindness/cruelty

   f. faith/disbelief

   g. family

   h. love/hate

   i. peace/war

   j. the American dream

   k. diversity

9. Knowing what you do about the author's life and times, explain what you think motivated her to write the book.

10. Quote a passage from the book that you find particularly memorable. Explain how the author made it memorable for you and name the literary devices that she employed to make it memorable. Examples of literary devices are alliteration, foreshadowing, hyperbole, imagery, repetition, irony, metaphor, meter, motif, onomatopoeia, parallelism, personification, pun, rhyme, sarcasm, simile and symbol.

11. Describe your reaction to the memoir and what about it caused you to react that way.

12. Why do you think the author included the epigraphs from the New

Testament and the Pirkei Avot, the Jewish Ethics of the Fathers?

13. Why do you think the author included the Epilogue, a memoir written by her father?

Words Remembered in Pieces of Someday

(ALPHABETIZED BY FIRST LETTER)

As fair art thou, my bonnie lass / So deep in luve am I And I will luve thee still, my dear / Till a' the seas gang dry...

—From "O my Luve's Like a Red, Red Rose," by Robert Burns

At dusk, at dawn and noon, I will grieve and He will hear my voice...

—From Psalm 55

Baby you can drive my car /Yes, I'm gonna be a star/ Beep beep, beep beep, yeah!...

—From "Drive my Car," by the Beatles

Barukh atah Adonai Elohaynu melekh ha-olam/ Kiy vanu vacharta v'otanu qidashta mikol ha'amiym...

—From the Shabbat evening prayer

But, soft! what light through yonder window breaks? / It is the east...

—From *Romeo and Juliet,* by William Shakespeare

Castelvetrano is a small farming town primarily concerned with woodworking and the cultivation of vines and olive trees...

—From *Michelin Sicily,* 1998

Castelvetrano seems to have been a Greek town, though it was refounded by the Romans, who settled a colony of retired soldiers on it and gave it its present name...

—From *Cadogan Sicily*, by Dana Facaros, Michael Pauls and Jon Eldan

Dear God, true source of light and wisdom, give me a keen understanding, a retentive memory, the ability to grasp things correctly...

—From "Student's Prayer," by Thomas Aquinas

Every morning / Every evening / Ain't we got fun? / Not much money / Oh but honey / Ain't we got fun?...

—From "Ain't We Got Fun," by Richard Whiting,
Gus Kahn, Raymond S. Egan

For lo! the days are hastening on... / When peace shall over all the earth / Its ancient splendors fling / And the whole world send back the song / Which now the angels sing...

—From "It Came Upon a Midnight Clear,"
by Edmund Hamilton Sears and Richard Storrs Willis

From grease to shine in half the time...

—The slogan for Joy dishwashing liquid

Have yourself a merry little Christmas / let your heart be light / From now on, our troubles will be out of sight...

—From "Have Yourself a Merry Little Christmas,"
by Hugh Martin and Ralph Blane

I believe that children are our future / Teach them well and let them lead the way / Show them all the beauty they possess inside...

—From "Greatest Love of All," by Michael Masser and Linda Creed

I can bring home the bacon / Fry it up in a pan / And never ever let you forget you're a man / 'Cause I'm a WOMAN...

—From "I'm a Woman," by Jerry Leiber and Mike Stoller

I confess to almighty God, and to you, my brothers and sisters, that I have sinned through my own fault...

—From the Confiteor

If happy little blue birds fly beyond the rainbow, why oh why can't I?

—From "Over the Rainbow," by Harold Arlen and E.Y. Harburg

I see you Mary in the garden / In the garden of a thousand sighs / There's holy pictures of our children / Dancin' in a sky filled with light...

—From "The Rising," by Bruce Springsteen

I went out to the hazel wood / Because a fire was in my head / And cut and peeled a hazel wand / And hooked a berry to a thread...

—From "The Song of Wandering Aengus," by William Butler Yeats

If you can keep your head when all about you / Are losing theirs and blaming it on you...

—From "If," by Rudyard Kipling

In the beginning, when God created the heavens and the earth, the earth was a formless wasteland, and darkness covered the abyss...

—From Genesis 1

I've always longed for adventure / To do the things I've never dared. And here I'm facing adventure / Then why am I so scared?...

—From "I Have Confidence," by Richard Rodgers and
Oscar Hammerstein II

Juiced on Mateus, just hanging loose. . .
> —Paraphrased from "Social Disease," by Elton John

Let there be peace on earth / And let it begin with me. . . / With God as our father / Brothers all are we / Let me walk with my brother / In perfect harmony. . .
> —From "Let There Be Peace on Earth," by Jill Jackson and Sy Miller

Little Jack Horner/ Sat in a corner. . .
> —From "Namby Pamby" by Henry Carey

I'm sorry, Suzie. I tried my best, but. . .You couldn't get it because you're not Santa. You're just a nice old man with whiskers. . .
> —From *Miracle on 34th Street*, by Valentine Davies

Never shall I forget the little faces of the children, whose bodies I saw turned into wreaths of smoke beneath a silent blue sky. . .
> —From *Night*, by Elie Wiesel

O God / Fear and trembling come upon me / Oh, that I had wings like a dove! /I would fly away and be at rest.
> —From Psalm 55

O! So shows a snowy dove trooping with crows / As yonder lady o'er her fellows shows. . .
> —From *Romeo and Juliet*, by William Shakespeare

O! that you were yourself; / But, love you are no longer yours. . .
> —From "Sonnet 13," by William Shakespeare

On the first day of Christmas, my true love gave to me. . .
—From "The Twelve Days of Christmas," by an unknown author

Once, New Year's Day had dominated my life. I knew my sins grieved the Eternal; I implored his forgiveness. . .
—From *Night*, by Elie Wiesel

Raindrops on roses. . .
—From "My Favorite Things," by Richard Rodgers and
Oscar Hammerstein II

See, I will send my messenger, who will prepare the way before me. Then suddenly the Lord you are seeking will come to his temple. . .
—From Malachi 3

Show a little faith there's magic in the night / You ain't a beauty but hey you're alright. . .
—From "Thunderoad," by Bruce Springsteen

Smile and the world smiles with you / Cry and you cry alone. . .
—Paraphrased from "Smile" by John Turner and Geoffrey Parsons

Someday girl, I don't know when, we're gonna get to that place / where we really want to go, and we'll walk in the sun. . .
—From "Born to Run," by Bruce Springsteen

That, which you may suppose the most potent to arrest my imagination, is actually the least: for what is not connected with her to me? and what does not recall her?. . .
—From *Wuthering Heights*, by Emily Brontë

The federal courts have traditionally adhered to the related doctrines of
res judicata and collateral estoppel. Under res judicata. . .
   —From *Allen v. McCurry,* by Supreme Court Justice Potter Stewart

Thy kingdom come, thy will be done, on Earth as it is in Heaven. . .
                         —From the Pater Noster

V'ahav'ta eit Adonai Elohekha b'khol l'vav'kha uv'khol naf'sh'kha
uv'khol m'odekha. / V'hayu had'varim ha'eileh asher anokhi m'tzav'kha
hayom al l'vavekha. . .
                             —From the Shema

Volare, oh oh / Cantare, oh oh oh oh / Let's fly way up to the clouds / Away
from the maddening crowds. . .
        —From "Volare," English lyrics by Michael Parish

Why, man, he doth bestride the narrow world / Like a Colossus, and we
petty men / Walk under his huge legs and peep about. . .
        —From *Julius Caesar,* by William Shakespeare

Wives should be subordinate to their husbands as to the Lord. . .
                       —From Ephesians 5

LaVergne, TN USA
01 October 2010
199258LV00003B/14/P